# WHEN THIS MASK OF FLESH IS BROKEN

The Story of an American Protestant Family

*To Richard and Kathleen,*
*When I hope will find this*
*novel-gothic saga of*
*interest.*

*David*

*June 24, 2019*

# DAVID A. HOLLINGER

outskirts press

"David Hollinger's spare but powerful book evokes more eloquently than anything I've read the experience of living on the parched prairie in the years of the Great Depression. The Calvary of drought, misfortune and illness that his grandparents, his father, his two uncles, and his aunt endured was as painful as anything foretold by the Bible in which they so fervently believed. As the sole member of the next generation, Hollinger is truly the only one who escaped to tell the tale."

— Adam Hochschild
Author of *King's Leopold's Ghost*

In this richly detailed and emotionally bracing memoir David Hollinger sets a new standard for the genre: writing an original family history in which the author shines as a probing researcher and a central character. But for a few small contingencies in his parents' narrative he might have lived an entirely different life. Heartbreaking and inspiring, I couldn't put this book down.

— Richard Wightman Fox
Author of *Jesus in America* and
*Reinhold Niebuhr*

In the hands of an experienced scholar, the research into the family of which he is a descendant has turned into a fascinatingly narrated account of lives in the American and Canadian 20th-century. David Hollinger's *When This Mask of Flesh is Broken* is an often melancholy history of striving and loss, of religious ministry, westward migration, and farming in adverse conditions. It is also a remarkable attempt to understand the equanimity of earlier generations whose fates come to life in these pages.

— Werner Sollors
Author of *Temptation of Despair*

"This is a story about the bonds of survival that join families in the midst of hardship—as well as the dark rifts of confusion and pain. That harrowing personal tale provides a lens onto something larger. Hollinger, one of America's premier historians of ideas, has turned his expertise and insight onto his own people to transform their story into an intimate account of an austere Protestant faith in the crucible of the Great Depression, a theological pioneer journey spanning the North American continent."

— Molly Worthen, contributing opinion writer at the *New York Times* and author of *Apostles of Reason: The Crisis of Authority in American Evangelicalism*

Several of my seminary students know that the distinguished American intellectual historian David Hollinger has deep family roots in the Church of the Brethren peoplehood. In *WhenThis Mask of Flesh is Broken*, we now have an intriguing window into the Hollinger family history. We theologians of culture know that ethnographies, biographies and family histories can be as rich as theological texts in manifesting possible existential and spiritual meaning. Reading Hollinger's narrative, we in the Anabaptist-Pietist heritage see traces of our own extended cultural and religious stories.

— Scott Holland is the Warren Slabaugh Professor of Theology & Culture at Bethany Theological Seminary in partnership with the Earlham School of Religion in Richmond, Indiana.

# Table of Contents

# Preface

"That's American gothic," friends have remarked when hearing even a little about my father's family history.

What most prompts this reaction is the image of an unpainted house on the Saskatchewan prairie in the 1920s with a silent, depressed mother confined to an upstairs room while her teenage daughter manages a kitchen without running water or electricity, her three sons brave temperatures of 40 below zero farming on what had been "virgin land," and her preacher husband focuses on serving a tiny congregation of sectarian Pietist-Anabaptists. Affecting, too, is my grandmother's being without a leg amputated by a local doctor in a rush after she developed gangrene from an infected toe my grandfather had neglected to treat.

Adding to the effect are my grandfather's bad business decisions, resulting in his sons having to work the land as virtual sharecroppers to Winnipeg bankers. A family that had owned land in North America since arriving in Pennsylvania in the 1730s found itself, two centuries later, with no land and barely a thousand dollars cash from an auction sale of their worldly goods. My father and his siblings scattered, yet continued to depend upon one another. Each bore the marks of the Canadian experience and its religious matrix until they died.

**The Hollinger house on Section 13, Merrington District, Kindersley, Saskatchewan. In front are two dogs, Rex and Fritzi, who appear in many of the family's photographs.**

Many families have histories even more dramatic and moving than this one. I would be less inclined to tell it but for two circumstances. First, I am the only child born to any of the Hollingers who spent their youth in this particular "little house on the prairie." My uncles did not have children, nor did my aunt. My father almost didn't, either. When he died in 1987 my mother suddenly informed me that I was the result of an unintended pregnancy. The whole saga would leave no one to know of it now were it not for the accident of my conception and my parents' inability in 1940 to even imagine abortion. Second, my father always struggled for greater voice than he felt he had achieved. Shortly before his death he told me that among the things about which he had hoped to say more was the story I now tell. When he was dying he asked my mother and me to include in the printed program for his memorial service what he described as "a poem memorized in youth and remembered as the years came and went." This poem by Francis Claiborne Mason has been virtually unknown since it was published in 1928. I found no clipping of it in my father's possessions. He wrote it out from memory at the age of 83. I recently located the book in which it was published. He had every word right.

> When this unchanging mask of
> flesh is broken,
> This body borne to bed
> Then shall we speak at last
> the long unspoken,
> ineffably fine words we
> would have said.

I know my own words are not "ineffably fine." But they will have to do.

This memoir of my father's family was originally intended for my children and grandchildren, and a handful of family friends. But several of them encouraged me to think also of a larger readership. I then sent an expanded draft to a wider circle of friends, many of whom offered additional encouragement, resulting in the publication now before you. Of the many who helped me understand what I was doing, and what its potential might be, I here thank only those whose specific comments on the text and whose encouragement to go forward proved the most helpful to me: Jon Butler, Charles Capper, Carol Clover, Curtis Freeman, Richard Fox, Adam Hochschild, Arlie Hochschild, Daniel Immerwahr, John Kaag, James Kloppenberg, Bruce Kuklick, Thomas Laqueur, Thomas Leonard, Marilyn McEntyre, Ronald Numbers, James

Sheehan, Yuri Slezkine, Werner Sollors, Frances Starn, Randolph Starn, and Robert Weiss. My greatest debt is to my wife of fifty-one years, Joan Heifetz Hollinger.

Although I never met Joan Didion, Norman McLean, or Wallace Stegner, my sense of what a family memoir could be has been shaped by Didion's *Where I was From*, McLean's *A River Runs Through It*, and Stegner's *Wolf Willow*. Stegner's account of his childhood in a small prairie town on the Montana-Saskatchewan border has been especially evocative. It describes an atmosphere more like what the Hollingers experienced during their Saskatchewan decades than any other work known to me. Also, as I wrote I became aware of how the Hollinger saga can be understood as a long, stutter-step enactment of what Didion calls "The Crossing," referring to the often epic struggle of getting a family from the east to California. McLean's account of growing up in Montana as the son of a Presbyterian minister was all the more heuristic because of a churchly component not prominent in the books by Didion and Stegner, but central to the life of the Hollingers.

About the churchly part of the Hollinger experience, I want to underscore its institutionally focused character. Churches and the communities around them were the primary setting for almost every life decision the Hollingers made. Faith, doctrine, and religious feeling were in the background, but churches defined the choices each of the Hollingers made about where to live at any time in their lives. This makes their story somewhat different from what we find in autobiographical and fictional writings about god-talking, spiritually anxious souls. Although my father and his siblings were "Christians," certainly, I never heard any of them make a point of describing themselves with that term. They were "church people." This was the key social category—the identity—I learned as a child.

I have described my own upbringing in a world that categorized everyone as either church people or not church people in an autobiographical essay, "Church People and Others," Chapter 8 of my book, *After Cloven Tongues of Fire* (Princeton University Press, 2013), 170-189.

Two other aspects of the story distinguish it from the stories of many other American Protestant families of the same period. One is the emotionally and socially crippling effect of anxiety about mental illness. This anxiety was not unusual in the early decades of the twentieth century, given popular ideas about the heritability of mental traits. But having a brother committed to an asylum and a mother so depressed she never spoke to any of her children, or to anyone else, from the time my father was ten years old, had devastating consequences. My grandmother, like the "madwoman in the attic" of literary lore, was confined to an upstairs room with "chronic melancholia" until she died.

The final aspect of the story I want to flag here is the experience of downward class mobility. Many contemporaries were doing better and better in the 1920s, even as they experienced the great transition from rural to urban life. The Hollingers went in the opposite direction, mostly as a result of my grandfather's unwise decisions and his apparent inability to conceive of what might be in the best interests of his sons and daughters apart from his own aspirations. After being hauled off to Saskatchewan and caught there in a downward economic spiral, the Rev. Albert Hollinger, Sr.'s children tried desperately to hang on to the culture they had absorbed in the prosperous and well-educated farming community of Gettysburg.

Berkeley, California
March 2019

# CHAPTER ONE

## Pennsylvania and The Brethren

**Just who were** the Hollingers, and what kind of existence did they have in Pennsylvania before their life-altering experiences in Canada? And what happened to them later on, as they tried to put behind them the aspects of their youth that now seem gothic? Why did my father have such a hard time finding voice?

Four individuals are the central characters in the story: my father, Albert, always called "Junior," his sister Annie, and his brothers, Roland and Charles.

Albert Hollinger, Jr. (1903-1987), was the fifth of the seven children born to Albert Hollinger, Sr. (1854-1932) and Annie Deardorff Hollinger (1862-1927). All descended from four "Pennsylvania Dutch" families that had resided in Pennsylvania since well before the American Revolution: the Deardorffs, the Dutreys, the Hollingers, and the Lotts. The "Dutch" in this common characterization of the "plain people" of Pennsylvania is an Anglicization of "Deutsch," the German word many German-speaking peoples used to describe themselves in their early years in America. For a family tree, see the Genealogical Appendix.

This photo of Junior, Annie, Roland, and Charles (left to right) was taken in 1935 in Chicago at a time of hope, when all had begun to organize their lives around Junior's plan to become a minister and continue a family tradition stretching back almost 200 years.

Junior shared the Canadian experience with his sister, Annie Adeline Hollinger (1905-2006), and two of his brothers, Charles Raymond Hollinger (1896-1991) and Roland Ellis Hollinger (1907-2000). Two other siblings did not go to Canada. Archie Reed Hollinger (1894-1946) and Edith Hollinger Fellenbaum (1898-1985), by remaining in Pennsylvania, had very different lives from the four siblings who accompanied their father to Canada. The seventh child, Paul Hollinger (1900-1901), died of spinal meningitis as a toddler. These seven had a half-brother, Jacob Hollinger (1877-1953), the only issue of my grandfather's first marriage, to Jennie Hollinger, who died when Jacob was a youth. Jacob, too, remained in the east, but was always much involved in the lives of his half-siblings.

The Hollingers were known even in the 18th century as a family of preachers in the German Baptist Brethren, a Pietist-Anabaptist sect that in 1908 renamed itself the Church of the Brethren. The Deardorffs, my grandmother's family, were originally Lutherans, but by the early 19th century some had become Brethren. The Deardorffs and the Hollingers were largely German speaking until well into the 19th century. I have an 1810, Philadelphia-printed edition of Martin Luther's German translation of the New Testament that the Deardorffs used for several decades. My maternal great-grandmother, Annie Lott Deardorff (1827-1924) was born into the Lott family, which traced its ancestry to a Huguenot woman who had escaped France with her children after the St. Bartholomew's Day Massacre of 1572. That woman's descendants resided first in Holland and then in England before migrating to America. The Lotts intermarried with Scotch-Irish Pennsylvanians and were mostly Presbyterians, although by the 1820s some had married into Brethren families. One of the Lotts, a "Captain Lott," was prominent in family lore for having served in George Washington's army.

The Deardorffs and the Hollingers were embedded in extensive kinship networks in Southeastern Pennsylvania. Letters and photographs from the first two decades of the 20th century show my father and his siblings in constant contact with cousins and aunts and uncles. There were Boyer cousins and Diehl cousins, whose genetic connection to the Deardorffs and the Hollingers I never learned. The Deardorff family was the most closely knit, and appears to have been somewhat more prosperous than the Hollinger clan. Especially prominent in the family circle was "Grandma Deardorff" (the Annie Lott Deardorff mentioned above) who was a daily reminder of the family's long rootedness in the local community. She also provided a link through oral tradition not only to Captain Lott and the Revolutionary War, but to the conflicts of the Protestant

Reformation. My father and his siblings heard her tell stories she had heard in the 1830s, conveying awareness that ancestors of theirs had been murdered by Catholics.

Gettysburg and the surrounding farms and orchards of Adams County constituted the chief geographic environment. The family had earlier moved several times to enable my grandfather to lead various Brethren congregations, including in Washington, D. C. There, in 1900, he founded what became one of the largest Brethren congregations in the region, the Washington City Church, which still exists at Fourth and North Carolina, Southeast. The Hollingers also resided briefly in Fairfax County, Virginia, where my father and his sister Annie were born. But their primary home before the great migration to Canada was a 170-acre farm to which the family moved in 1905, located just north of the town of Gettysburg, straddling Carlisle Pike (now state route 34), along the tracks of the Reading Railroad. The farm was diversified, in keeping with the norm in that area; some crops and livestock were for commercial sale, but the Hollingers grew their own produce, maintained their own stock of milk cows, and butchered their own pork and beef. Not far away was the even more substantial Deardorff farm, maintained by my grandmother's family.

The Hollinger farm was on soil that had been part of the Confederate line on the first day of the Battle of Gettysburg. The children were acutely aware of having grown up on the famous battlefield. The family collected dozens of bullets turned up by their horse drawn plows. Most of these heavy mementos were discarded as the family moved to Canada and beyond. Two were saved, one Union, one Confederate, and were eventually left to me. My grandmother, as a one-year-old, was held in the arms of a Union cavalry officer while her mother—the Grandma Deardorff mentioned above—drew

This map shows the location of the Hollinger farm just north of town. The farm straddled Carlisle Pike, later Highway 34. A portion of Gettysburg National Battlefield Park now embraces what had been the southernmost segment of the Hollinger property.

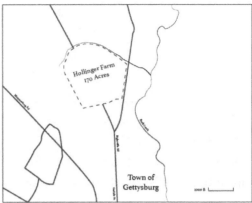

Hollinger Farm
170 Acres

Town of
Gettysburg

1000 ft

water for his company at the Deardorff farm, several miles distant from town. Later, as a young woman, my grandmother was named "Daughter of the Regiment" at the 1889 reunion of the Sixteenth Pennsylvania Cavalry. Several of the veterans recalled their 1863 visit to the Deardorff farm. The Hollingers witnessed the fiftieth anniversary celebration of the battle in 1913. Charles, who at 17 was old enough to absorb details, once told me he had seen in the flesh "the hero of Little Round Top," Col. Joshua Chamberlin of the legendary Twentieth Maine.

None of the Hollingers or Deardorffs served in the military. The Brethren were, like the Mennonites and Quakers, strict pacifists. Refusal of military service was still the norm for Brethren during World War I. Charles would have refused induction had he been called, but farm workers were then exempt if they chose to be. Charles' government-issued card from 1917 records that classification for him. Archie, who was an ordained minister even though working as a teacher, was exempt as a clergyman. Junior and Roland were too young. Later, during World War II, Roland was the only one of the Hollinger men still young enough to be drafted. He became a conscientious objector and performed four years of alternative service.

Growing up Brethren in early-twentieth-century Pennsylvania meant above all being part of a tight community that got along well enough with other Protestants but was still heavily tribal. The Brethren saw themselves as a particular people who were obliged by circumstances to deal with members of other confessions and with civil authority, but only at a certain distance. Founded in Germany in 1708, the "Dunkers," as the Brethren were popularly known because of their insistence on baptism by triune immersion (in keeping with Matthew 28:19: baptism was to be carried out "in the name of the Father, and of the Son, and of the Holy Ghost"), were overwhelmingly rural. They espoused what they called "the simple life," and declared the New Testament to be their only creed, thereby expressing the standard Pietist antipathy to sharply defined doctrines. Preachers like my grandfather made theological pronouncements in sermons, but what most defined the community was a set of rules for living and worshiping. Doing baptism correctly mattered greatly. Swearing was proscribed, so if one was asked in court to swear to tell the truth, one said "I so affirm." Meeting houses had no steeples, which were understood to display an absence of humility of spirit. At regular "love feasts," church members washed one another's feet (John 13:14: "If I then, your Lord and Master, have washed your feet; ye also ought to wash one another's feet"). Lutherans and Presbyterians were not enemies, but they were too worldly. They did not wash one another's feet. They celebrated Christmas. Junior and his siblings did not observe Christmas until their father died in 1932. Dressing plainly was very important, especially for women.

The one rule for conduct that most affected the family during the years prior to the move to Canada was a provision in the prevailing dress code for women. Like most of the "plain people" (notably, the Amish and the Brethren in Christ in addition to the Mennonites and the Church of the Brethren), the Brethren required baptized women to cover their heads. A white "prayer covering" often sufficed, but many Brethren congregations, including the one in Gettysburg, required a black bonnet. For refusing to wear the bonnet, my father's sister Edith, at the age of 15, was "churched"—the term used for being expelled from full membership. It is not clear what Albert Hollinger, Sr., thought about this, but Edith told me that her father had not tried to stop several women in the local congregation who were determined to cast out the senior minister's daughter. Edith had fallen in with the local Lutheran and Presbyterian girls. She was not interested in reminding everyone

of her sect. The church ladies called her to heel, and when she ignored them they persuaded the congregation to throw her out. She remained in the Hollinger household but spent more and more time with Presbyterians, eventually marrying one (Austin Fellenbaum, 1899-1944) without her father's approval. Edith herself was proudly Presbyterian for the rest of her life.

**Edith at 17, two years after she was expelled from the Gettysburg Church of the Brethren for refusing to wear a prescribed head-covering.**

Paternal approval is something Archie always enjoyed. His social and cultural trajectory reveals the community's greater tolerance for males who kept company with non-Brethren. From an early age Archie was relieved of most farm chores in order to pursue his studies. After finishing Gettysburg College in 1916, he spent a summer at the University of Chicago studying English literature, and in 1917-1918 earned an M. A. at George Washington University. Along the way, he was ordained to the Brethren ministry. He did some preaching, but never had the responsibility of leading a church and was always employed as a teacher at high schools and academies. His photographs show a snappily dressed figure with a proud countenance, more urbane than his brothers in comparable photos.

**Archie with the family's 1919 Studebaker in Gettysburg in 1921.**

The Hollinger family's class position was relatively strong within the rural population of Brethren in Southeastern Pennsylvania. Despite the conflict over Edith's refusal to wear the bonnet, the family was on relaxed social terms with the local Lutherans and Presbyterians. The Lutheran president and faculty of Gettysburg College and Academy corresponded regularly with Charles and Annie after they moved to Canada. The Hollingers were not rich, but they were not poor. Archie's access to higher education and teaching jobs was consistent with their social position.

It was during these Gettysburg years that my grandmother's depression took hold. How, why, and precisely when it began is not clear. It was never discussed when I was growing up. I did not learn of it until I was 27, in 1968, when my somewhat renegade Aunt Edith decided that it was time I learned about it. My father described it only once, when I told him what I had learned from Edith. All he could say before weeping was "Well, she broke in one day," and from that moment, she never spoke to him again. He was not yet eleven when this happened. I did not ask him about it again. He did open the topic shortly before his death but immediately found himself unable to speak. After he died in 1987, Annie and Roland proved more willing to talk about the painful parts of the family's history. I asked each of them what their father said to them about their mother's illness, and the reply was "nothing." Your father did not talk with you about this, helping you to understand it, I pressed? "No," both said, in separate conversations. I persisted: so, you children just dealt with this by yourselves? "Yes."

What did happen? Edith was away at Blue Ridge Academy, a Brethren school just across the Maryland line. Her mother was "just fine" when Edith went off to school, following a visit home in March 1914. When she returned for the summer, her mother was simply "gone." The most complete account is Annie's recollection when in her eighties. She and Roland had gone down to the well to fetch buckets of water, and played there for a few minutes before returning to the house. Their mother scolded them mildly for their tardiness, as the water was needed in the kitchen. It was their last conversation. Annie Deardorff Hollinger soon walked into her room without any announcement, and said nothing more. From that moment the children were cared for by "Auntie" (Adeline Hollinger), their father's unmarried sister, who had already moved into their home.

There is no way of knowing what modern therapies might have accomplished for my grandmother. Edith believed that sheer exhaustion was a factor in her illness. She had experienced eleven pregnancies in a span of fourteen years, including four miscarriages in addition to the seven live births. Two of the children, Annie and Roland, were born after their mother was partially paralyzed as a result of Junior's complicated birth in 1903. Even after his physically impaired wife was hobbling around, trying in her forties to manage the children and the household, her husband impregnated her twice more.

But there may be more to it. Edith told me that Archie during those years was a secret homosexual and that their mother understood this and was troubled by it. There had been incidents with other youths when Archie was a student, according to Edith, and one of them had taken his own life. Edith believed that Archie later moved from one job to another—Littletown, Hershey, Dillsburg, then Blue Ridge within a span of six years—on account of incidents with students that were "hushed up" because of his father's high standing throughout the region. I am not sure what to make of Edith's representation of Archie. Only she ever said anything about his apparent sexual orientation and attendant scandals. But only she, of all the siblings, was worldly enough to be comfortable with the topic. Edith's credibility is enhanced by her accounts of other aspects of the family history; what she told me about everything else is consistent with the letters and other documents that survive. Moreover, Archie behaved in increasingly bizarre ways immediately after most of the family left for Canada. As I detail below, he was committed to an asylum from 1922 until his death twenty-four years later. His few surviving letters from 1916 and 1917 are highly intelligent and reveal an engagement with contemporary world affairs unusual in the family correspondence.

My grandmother's difficulties thus remain something of a mystery, as do Archie's. But the setting for both of these mysteries, and for everything else, changed dramatically in 1921 with the move to

Canada. Archie and Jacob remained in the East, as did Edith, who by then had earned her B. A. from Gettysburg College and begun teaching elementary school. At twenty-three, Edith was also planning to marry. Edith's boyfriend, Austin, boarded the train to speak to her father before it departed, saying "I want you to know that I intend to marry your daughter." The Dunker patriarch replied only, "Figured as much." He did not put out his hand to shake Austin's.

Why the departure from Gettysburg? Why to Saskatchewan?

**This family portrait was taken in 1913, a year before my grandmother's depression began. Archie, Edith, and Charles are in back. Annie and Junior are in front. In the middle row are my grandfather, Roland, my grandmother, and half-brother Jacob.**

# CHAPTER TWO

## Canada and Continual Crisis

**The early twentieth** century was still within the age of the "free ministry" for most Anabaptist and Pietist communions. Preachers were not salaried employees but fulfilled pastoral obligations while making their livings and supporting their families independently, usually as farmers. Most congregations had several men who had been called to the ministry by parishioners because they had leadership skills and mastery of the sect's defining doctrines and rules. Larger congregations often sought out gifted preachers and tried to persuade them to move. When invited to lead a new congregation, it was not unusual for preachers to consider whether the move included an opportunity to acquire better land.

Land and religion fit together easily in western Canada because several hundred Brethren had migrated there in response to the opening of that domain by the Canadian Pacific Railway.

Countless letters and magazine articles heralded the new agricultural and religious frontier, where, it was said, wheat grew abundantly and the pioneers were much in need of religious leadership. My grandfather read these reports in *The Gospel Messenger* (the Brethren weekly) and elsewhere, and came to believe that on the

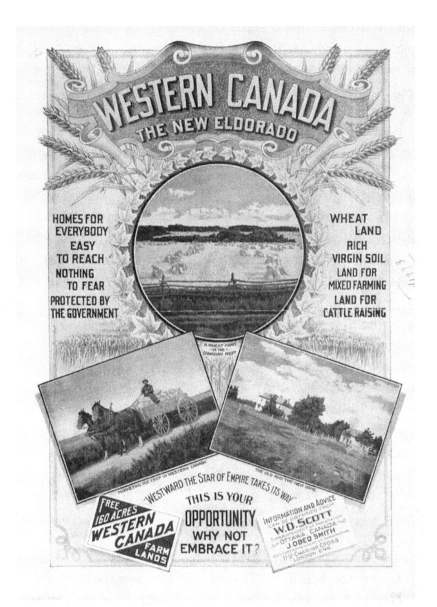

This flyer is typical of the promotional literature distributed by the Canadian Pacific Railway and its affiliated land agents.

Canadian prairies he could obtain a large enough piece of land to eventually distribute sizeable holdings to Charles, Junior, and Roland, all of whose future in farming was never questioned. Of the male children in this strictly patriarchal family, Archie alone had been assigned a different track.

Without consulting even his older children about the move he was contemplating, my grandfather toured Saskatchewan and Alberta in the summer of 1920, visiting several churches and evaluating options for purchasing land. Most of the Brethren were in southern Alberta. But a new opportunity arose when my grandfather received an invitation from a dissident faction of the Brethren in Christ congregation at Kindersley, in the far west of Saskatchewan about 200 miles north of Havre, Montana. The Kindersley dissidents were unhappy with a turn toward Pentecostalism by another faction, and wanted to break away. The Brethren in Christ denomination was an offshoot of the Mennonites, following a schism in 1760s Pennsylvania, and, while definitely kindred to the Church of the Brethren, was understood to be more conservative. The Brethren in Christ were often called "River Brethren," following their commitment, like the "Dunkers," to triune immersion baptism performed in a river. When the anti-Pentecostal group of Brethren in Christ heard that the illustrious Pennsylvania preacher was pondering a move to Canada and was traveling nearby, it offered to merge with the Church of the Brethren if he would join them.

The invitation came with a solid church edifice, the oldest in that part of the province, built in 1910 by the first settlers and controlled by the dissidents whose ranks included some of the most prosperous farmers in the area. My grandfather might not have accepted the invitation had he not been urged to do so by his distant cousin, David Hollinger of Redcliffe, Alberta, who was then the primary leader of the Church of the Brethren in Western Canada and had visited Kindersley and preached there. My grandfather agreed to lead a "fusion" congregation at "the Merrington church," as it was called, referring to the farming community where it was located. He purchased one full section (640 acres) that had been farmed for several years, and a half-section (320 acres) that had never been "broken," as the first cultivation was then called. The move as presented to the children felt like "a great adventure," a genuine "frontier experience," my father once explained to me when I expressed puzzlement at a move away from a successful farm in one of the finest agricultural regions of the world. The great myth of "Virgin Land" was part of the mystique. But what most drove the decision was my grandfather's eagerness to exercise religious leadership in what appeared to be a bourgeoning society. He liked to say he had heard "the Macedonian Call," a reference to Acts 16:9, where the Apostle Paul described a vision in which he was approached by a man from Macedonia, saying to him, "Come over to Macedonia and help us."

My grandfather, like many others who purchased land in Saskatchewan and Alberta around that time, was entirely oblivious to the long-standing conclusion of agricultural economists that one large portion of those two provinces was too dry for sustained, successful farming. Kindersley is well within "Palliser's Triangle," a region of southwestern Saskatchewan and southeastern Alberta named for a surveyor who reported his negative findings in 1858. John Palliser treated the US border as the bottom of a triangle, the other sides of which ran northwest through central Saskatchewan (the provinces were not established and named until 1905) and northeast through central Alberta to join at a point about 130 miles north of Kindersley, where the town of Lloydminster now straddles the border of the two provinces. But in 1920, Palliser's analysis was widely disregarded on account of the good weather of the previous decade, and perhaps more importantly, because the Canadian Pacific Railroad vigorously promoted land purchases and even employed some churchmen as agents of the Railroad. Among those who worked with the Railroad was my grandfather's cousin David Hollinger, who so strongly urged the move to Kindersley.

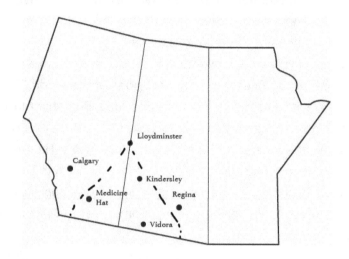

**The dotted line on this map indicates the shape of Palliser's Triangle. Palliser distinguished degrees of aridity. He found the most arid area to run from Kindersley south to the Montana line, east to Vidora, and west to Medicine Hat.**

The family traveled to Kindersley by train, arriving at the end of March in order to plant that season's crop of wheat. The Hollinger party of 1921 consisted of my 67-year-old grandfather, my 59-year-old grandmother, the four children (Charles, Junior, Annie, and Roland), and Auntie, who had been in charge of their household for the previous seven years. I do not know if my grandmother was aware of how big a decision this was. My grandfather apparently believed that the move made no difference to his withdrawn wife. Perhaps it did not. My father once managed to say he thought his mother was by then beyond having an opinion about it. But in Gettysburg she was surrounded by the extended Deardorff clan and many friends within the area's network of flourishing Brethren congregations. According to Edith, her mother was able to recognize some of her relatives and friends when they visited. Nothing like that awaited her in Kindersley. Edith believed that whatever chance there may have been for recovery was lost with the departure from Gettysburg.

The Merrington church in 1921, when my grandfather took over pastoral duties.

Physically, the new country was flat. At sunrise or sunset a boy could see his own shadow a mile long, noted Wallace Stegner hyperbolically in *Wolf Willow*, his memoir of a childhood spent not that far south of where the Hollingers lived.

**This picture, despite the camera's not having been held level, shows the flat prairie just after it was broken on the Hollinger farm, northeast of Kindersley.**

In a sketch she wrote more than twenty years later, Annie recalled how bleak and barren the prairie environment seemed from the moment the family arrived. There were hardly any trees, and many of the dwellings were sod houses, built by the first pioneers from blocks of soil carved from the earth and stacked on top of one another. There were wooden houses, too, built after the completion of the railroad made it easier to bring in lumber. But these homes were "out there very much alone and unprotected," with no woods around them. Annie recalled, too, the nostalgia for the Pennsylvania farm that was an enduring emotion during all of their years in Canada:

> We thought often of that old farm which yielded most of the food needed for a big family. We sometimes wished we could walk up to the orchard and gather the peaches, apples, pears, crabapples, and quinces which grew there. And how nice it would be to go out in the woods again and pick the raspberries, blackberries, huckleberries, and elderberries which grew

there! Then too there were those big butcherings, when several hogs and maybe a beef were made into countless yards of sausage and into hams, bacon, and shoulders. These last three were sugar-cured and hung in the smoke-house to be smoked over hickory-wood smoke. These things we missed.

Several features of the new life on the prairies soon established themselves. Charles led the farming operation. At 25, he had already taken over much of the Gettysburg farm as his aging father devoted himself more exclusively to church affairs. Charles was the only one of the four children to have completed high school. He had also attended Gettysburg College episodically, but he seems to have been easily persuaded to make the move to Canada. Annie and Roland attended high school in Kindersley for part of that first year, but they soon joined Charles and Junior in farm and household work. Back in Gettysburg, Junior had attended some high school, and would have finished had the family remained there. But in Canada he was in the fields with Charles from the moment the family arrived.

During the first year, Auntie worked with Annie in the kitchen, but she was not happy with the primitive conditions. She returned to Gettysburg in 1922. This left Annie, at 17, in charge. Annie ran the family kitchen and did the housekeeping for the next sixteen years.

Only after 1924 did the Hollingers reside on their own farmland. During their first three years, they rented dwellings on adjacent farms or in the town of Kindersley. Then my grandfather learned of an abandoned house eleven miles from town. He purchased it and had it hauled to the family's farm by a 30-60 Rumley tractor, a huge kerosene-burning, heavy-steel tractor often used to break the prairie, and indeed the same one the family hired to break

Charles during his first summer on the prairie.

Annie and Roland on the prairie shortly after their arrival in Canada.

part of section 13. The house was cramped. Junior and Roland often slept in an adjacent cook-house that had no heat. They slept in layers of long underwear and thick woolen caps and under heavy covers. But on many mornings their breath had frozen so hard on the nearest blanket that a cake of ice could be peeled off and thrown to the floor and smashed. Kerosene lamps and battery-powered electrical units lit the house.

Junior in the early 1920s, in Kindersley.

Moreover, there was no water on the Hollinger property. Once the house was in place, my grandfather hired a driller whose apparatus went 185 feet deep but, to everyone's surprise, the drill never reached water. Snow melt provided some water pumped into troughs for the horses and the dogs, but the family hauled their drinking and cooking water from town throughout their remaining years in that house. My grandfather had purchased the driest land in the vicinity.

In the meantime, in August of 1921 the farm suffered a crippling economic blow from which the family never recovered. A ferocious hailstorm destroyed their first crop of wheat before it could be harvested. It was a splendid crop, estimated at 35 bushels per acre. Anything above 30 bushels per acre was considered a very good crop. Hail stones as large as golf balls came down in torrents. Charles, who was out driving in the family's 1919 Studebaker, crawled under the car for safety and discovered, upon emerging, that the car's thick canvas top had been shredded. But what made the storm a disaster was that my grandfather had not bought hail insurance. He had been strongly advised to do so. Hailstorms were common on the Canadian prairies. Other farmers routinely insured their crops. I suspect he "trusted in the Lord," although the family always said only that he had been "too tight" to buy insurance. The farm earned no income that year. What savings the family had were quickly depleted by basic living expenses.

Thus began the family's economic decline and their downward social mobility, in the swirl of which, my father and his siblings struggled to hold on to the culture they had inherited from the relatively well-positioned Gettysburg Brethren.

The next year brought little relief. The season was dry. Without rain, the crop was thin. Worse, the great agricultural depression of the 1920s had begun, and the world market for wheat was so poor that the family earned little from the wheat they did harvest. They also raised some barley, flax, and oats, but wheat was then and always the main crop. With two bad years behind him, my grandfather sought financial relief. The two local parties from whom he had purchased the full section, and to whom he still owed most of the purchase price, were unwilling to make adjustments. My grandfather kept these creditors at bay and handled living expenses by borrowing a thousand dollars from a prosperous Brethren farmer in Medicine Hat, Alberta. At the time, everyone assumed this debt would soon be repaid. But I learned from Charles' correspondence that, as late as 1942, Charles, who had inherited the debt, was still chipping away at it, paying a few dollars a year to the friendly but frustrated family acquaintance.

In dealing with the Winnipeg bank that held the mortgage on the half-section, my grandfather asked the assistance of the officials of the Canadian Pacific Railroad who had urged his migration. The railroad men wrote to the Winnipeg bank and arranged for slightly better terms. They explained to the bankers that the Rev. Hollinger was an important figure, and had persuaded his denomination to hold its annual assembly in Calgary that summer. Many hundreds of Brethren would be riding the rails from Pennsylvania, Ohio, and Indiana and staying in the hotels of Alberta's finest city. That much was true. At the Church's Annual Conference in Indiana the year before, my grandfather had delivered an apparently inspiring speech about the glories of western Canada and the great future for church work there. The official request of the District of Western Canada to host the conference, almost certainly written by my grandfather, expressed a hearty confidence:

> The Church of the Brethren here feels that it has an unlimited field, and it also realizes a special call to occupy it. It feels that its call is just as real and true as that of Abraham when God said: "Get thee out of thy country and from thy kindred and come until the land which I will show thee."

The 1923 Annual Conference was duly held in Calgary. Brethren from congregations all over the United States attended. Yet, many of the delegates voiced a concern that some of the Canadian Brethren were more interested in real estate profiteering than in spreading the gospel. So far as I know, this charge was not made specifically against my grandfather, although it might have been.

The Rev. Albert Hollinger, Sr.'s stature as a church leader was widely recognized. The Brethren in Christ, with whom the Brethren in Kindersley remained affiliated, named him the Bishop of Western

Canada. He liked to have his leadership recognized and treasured the title, for which there was no equivalent in the Church of the Brethren. While he was a bishop only in his Brethren in Christ persona, he was also the principal leader of the Canadian Churches of the Brethren after cousin David Hollinger moved back to Ohio, his earlier home. My grandfather put a good face on the challenges of the Kindersley scene, as in this report of a Sunday morning church service he sent to the *Gospel Messenger* in January 1928:

> I drove seven miles in a sleigh today to meet with our congregation and serve them, the thermometer forty degrees below zero. We are learning to endure the hardship as we go forward toward the setting of the sun... The warm hearts of our dear brethren and sisters and the many dear little children who attend services these cold Sundays richly compensate us for what we suffer from the cold and somehow the Lord makes us feel our sacrifice and service are not in vain.

Before the Hollingers arrived, the weather had been good and so too, had been the market. Families who had settled there soon after the railroad reached Kindersley in 1909 profited from a series of anomalously wet years and from the exceptionally great demand for wheat during World War I. Families who had enriched themselves during the 1910s were better able to get through the dry weather and poor markets of the 1920s. They paid very little for their land and typically carried no debt. The Hollingers arrived after the boom was over, yet before the cost of land had declined. My grandfather paid fifty dollars per acre for the section already broken and forty dollars per acre for the half section that had yet to be broken. He paid about ten times as much for his land as the settlers of a decade before had paid for theirs.

Still, the farming proceeded year after year. I have some striking photographs of the wheat fields, the tractors, and the threshing equipment the Hollingers used.

**The 60-110 Case Steam Engine Tractor the Hollingers frequently rented from their friend, Isaac Baker.**

**Junior is at far left of this photo of the threshing crew of 1926, which shows how prominent horses still were in the process.**

**Charles to the left, then Junior, along with the men they hired for threshing. Roland is third from right, in the back. This picture is from about 1930.**

At harvest time the Hollingers hired seasonal workers and Annie was assisted in the kitchen by girls and young women from the community. A few harvests were so good that Charles kept small bottles of wheat kernels from those years, suitably labelled. He gave them to me shortly before he died at the age of 94. They did have hail insurance every year after 1922, but there was no protection against the dust storms, early frosts, and pests that often damaged the crops. A great novel about prairie life has etched in popular memory the destruction that a horde of locusts could wreak. "The demons left behind them evil enough to pollute a whole continent," wrote O. E. Rolvagg in *Giants in the Earth,* describing the total destruction of wheat crops by this classically Biblical plague. Against these hazards there was no shield but luck. Letters and dated photographs are reminders that heavy snows and bitter cold sometimes struck as early as mid-October. Even when the weather and other circumstances produced a bountiful yield, the market remained poor. The family was never able to paint the house.

**A blurry photo of Junior and Charles with horses outside the house after an unseasonably early blizzard of October 12, 1930.**

Not until the end of 1924, several years after radios became a vital link between prairie farms and the outside world, did the Hollingers purchase one to help them get through the long winter days and evenings. There was always pressure to give whatever money they had to their creditors. My grandfather's journal for the first five months of 1923 describes one drab and silent day after another, often mentioning that he was left alone for the evening while his four children went to another home to sing hymns with other young people. This, and church, were their primary diversions. In the winter, my father and his brothers spent many hours curling on the ice, a sport then little known in the United States but popular in the ice rinks found in almost every Saskatchewan town. Skating on the lakes and rivers was another popular sport. When not frozen over, the rivers were often used for baptisms.

**My grandfather baptizing Roland in the South Saskatchewan River in July 1923.**

In the early years Charles was not sure he wanted to remain part of the Canadian enterprise. He went east for the winters of 1921-22, 1923-24 and 1925-26, earning what he could in odd jobs around Gettysburg. During his first winter east, Charles wrote a letter to the family that elicited an anxious reply from Junior. In what is his only surviving letter from all of his years in Canada, Junior on January 26, 1922, describes a bleak scene and implores Charles to return:

> You seem to be throwing the hint that you will try to stay shy of this place this summer. We would be very much dis-appointed if you would not come and stay with us at least another year till we get things in better shap[e]. Dad worries quite a bit since we moved because he has nothing at all to keep his mind off his troubles. He just walks back and forth through the house, groaning most of the time. He walks out about once or twice a week... Last Sunday it was 50 below

zero, and the roads were drifted full of snow, so we could not go out to church.

Before the letter was mailed, my grandfather, who undoubtedly had authorized it, scribbled on it a plea of his own to Charles: "I would not know how to get along without you this summer. If you boys stay by me for another year or two, I think we can come out better."

Charles did return for the summer of 1922 and kept coming back year after year, but he and Edith and Jacob corresponded among themselves about what his future should be. Edith visited Kindersley in the summer of 1922 and concluded that the Canadian venture was a mistake. A few months after her visit she wrote Charles that she would try to find a way to re-purchase the Gettysburg farm if Charles would bring the family home. She had a candid relationship with Charles and sometimes complained to him of their father's "narrowness." Charles did not pursue his sister's "strictly private" (as she wrote on the envelope for this letter) suggestion. Jacob was no less skeptical. Several times he assured Charles that the loyal son had done his share for the family and might well pursue his own fortunes back in Pennsylvania. I do not know why Charles chose the path he did, but I suspect that the vulnerability of his parents and his younger siblings weighed heavily upon him.

During these years that Charles was going back back and forth, several events in Kindersley affected the family deeply. One was the behavior of Archie. Jacob learned in the fall of 1922 that Archie was no longer teaching at Blue Ridge Academy. He wrote Charles asking if he knew where Archie was. Charles did not know, either. Edith wrote Charles that she had received some odd letters from their brother. Then, without advance notice, Archie showed up at the Hollinger farm. He soon proved "unmanageable," as it was put in the family's letters. My grandfather was unwilling to act, but after several weeks, Charles consulted with a local doctor and took it upon himself to have his brother committed. Charles authorized police officers to confine Archie and transport him to the Saskatchewan provincial hospital for the mentally ill at North Battleford. There is no detailed account of just what Archie had done, but Jacob and Edith both wrote to Charles to assure him he was correct and courageous to go around their father to act as he did. The elder Hollinger may never have been at peace with what had happened to his favorite child. He wrote to Charles a few years later, saying it pained him that Archie was writing to him from the asylum, complaining of having been "taken away in chains." He had been.

The traumatic scene with Archie repeated itself in 1927. The troubled son and brother appeared again in Kindersley. This was all the more remarkable because by then Archie had been transferred to the Pennsylvania state asylum in Harrisburg. After the government of Saskatchewan had been billing the family for the costs of confining of a non-citizen, my grandfather in 1925 persuaded the Pennsylvania authorities to take Archie as a US citizen and a resident of Pennsylvania. As in Saskatchewan, his confinement was involuntary. The Harrisburg asylum's still-existing case file records that Archie "escaped" and was then re-committed. The family was never clear on how he got away and managed to get across the country and cross the border. Charles tolerated Archie's presence for weeks that became months, hoping that Archie would prove able to function within the family setting, but it did not work. One day Charles hired the local blacksmith—the strongest man around—to subdue Archie until the police could again take custody of him and arrange his return to Harrisburg. Again, he was taken away in chains. Archie remained confined in the Harrisburg asylum until his death in 1946.

This photo of the Hollinger men was taken in **1927**, at the time Jacob visited for my grandmother's funeral. From left, my grandfather, Jacob, Junior, Charles, and Roland. Archie was not included in this photo, although he was in Kindersley.

The asylum's files list Archie's diagnosis as "dementia praecox, simple type." Edith told me Archie was "schizophrenic," a term the Harrisburg staff may have used in their conversations with her during her occasional visits. Jacob, too, visited Archie periodically and would sometimes refer to Archie's condition as "unchanged" in letters to Charles. Junior saw Archie for the last time during what turned out to be his own last trip to Pennsylvania, in 1932. Roland and Charles last visited Archie in 1935.

However Archie's behavior might be diagnosed by a psychiatrist today, there is no doubt what his condition meant to his siblings. Having a brother with such serious emotional problems froze in his brothers and sisters whatever capacity they might have had to overcome the terror produced by their mother's illness in the absence of any interpretative framework other than the popular genetic lore of the age. Edith did have one child, Anne Fellenbaum

Bacon (1928-2000), but Edith told me that she had never been free of the worry that she would eventually "get melancholia like mother." Charles married at the age of 47 and had no children. When my mother revealed the unintended nature of the pregnancy that resulted in my own birth, she explained that it was my father's profound anxiety about his mother and brother that led to their decision not to have children. Annie and Roland never married. I once asked Roland if Annie as a young woman ever had boyfriends. He said no. "All those years in Canada, she never dated," I asked. He insisted she had not, even though, as her photos reveal, she was a beautiful young woman. Roland explained: "We were always afraid."

**Annie is seated next to a local youth in his roadster in 1931.**

Roland, as the youngest and the most significantly deprived of normal parenting, was traumatized by a dramatic public event in Kindersley. In the summer of 1924, my grandfather arranged for a series of revival meetings led by a Nebraska-based Brethren evangelist. Florid altar calls and circus-like preaching missions were never common among the Brethren, but in the 1920s the denomination did have a handful of stereotypically hell-fire revivalists who held meetings periodically in given districts. The flamboyant preacher attracted large crowds. His meetings were held in the local ice skating rink and brought eighty new members into the church. Nearly all of them soon dropped out. But the sensitive Roland, not yet 17, was frightened by the evangelist's vivid representations of hell and the community's apparent approval of his view of the world. In his eighties Roland described the 1924 revival as the most psychologically traumatic event of his youth. "I was convinced that I was going to hell," he explained. Roland decided to kill himself. He walked out into the prairies looking for a large rock with which to strike his head. He did not find one. He walked home in confusion. He said nothing about this episode to anyone, not even his siblings. He dealt privately with the psychological legacy of the event for a number of years, reliving in memory his suicide attempt. He told me I was the first and only person to whom he had described the experience, seventy years after the fact.

Roland's siblings were able to keep the evangelist's preachments in perspective. None of them mentioned the revival to me except as a weird spectacle that they—especially my father—were embarrassed to admit their church had sanctioned. Several years after the meetings in Saskatchewan, the evangelist was defrocked upon being discovered *flagrante* with a married woman in his Nebraska congregation.

Roland was also disoriented that same year when his mother's leg was amputated. As she was recovering, family members took turns sitting in her Kindersley hospital room. When his initial turn came, it was the first time he had been alone with his mother since her depression had taken hold a decade before, when he was six years old. Her confinement was such that her own son, living in the same house all those years, had never entered her room unaccompanied. She was physically cared for by her husband. After the operation she was impassive and heavily drugged, but Roland felt the enormous weight of his mother's suffering for the first time. He fled the hospital, simply overwhelmed by the magnitude of it all, and began to walk from the town out onto the prairie. But his father sent for him. They found him walking alone and guided him back to his mother's room. It was his turn. There was no escape.

My grandmother died three years later. Her gravestone can be seen today in a treeless cemetery next to the spot where her husband's church once stood. "Sacred to the memory of Annie Deardorff, Beloved wife of Bishop Albert Hollinger, 1862-1927," it reads, and then quotes Revelation 14:13: "Blessed are the dead which die in the Lord."

**My grandmother's gravestone at the Merrington Cemetery when I visited there in 1990.**

The children were surprised that their father wanted his own title as bishop included on the gravestone, another sign, surely, of his own self-importance. Jacob and Edith both traveled to Kindersley for the funeral. My grandmother's obituary in the *Gospel Messenger* was written by C. D. Bonsack, a national figure in the Church of the Brethren. Bonsack described the deceased as "a woman of much more than ordinary ability and talents," who had been "a most delightful conversationalist" until an "affliction" had made her "a great sufferer" for the last thirteen years of her life.

With my grandmother gone, the family could more easily spend the winter months in Pennsylvania. Until then, only Charles had done so. Now they all went, first in 1929-30, then in 1931-32. They drove east in November, and returned in late March. In Pennsylvania, my grandfather spoke in many churches and at various conferences while his children worked in odd jobs. Junior was employed in the potato chip factory of his Uncle Adam, one of his father's brothers. Their base was Lancaster, where Edith lived with her husband Austin and infant daughter Anne. Austin was financially ruined in the crash of 1929. Edith began running a kindergarten that became her family's chief source of income for a number of years.

Annie kept an "Autographs" book during these years in which messages of good will were written by the friends with whom they socialized both in Pennsylvania and Canada. In keeping with convention, these entries frequently include quotations from scripture or uplifting poetry, mixed with expressions of pleasure at having spent time with Annie and her family. My eye is caught by an entry made by Edith. "It's not fair to be the one that's left behind." Another that catches my eye was written in Gettysburg on February 16, 1930, by Francis Mason, the poet whose verses my father had memorized.

**Photograph taken in 1932 in front of Edith's house in Lancaster. Left to right, Junior, Roland, Annie, Edith, Charles, and Jacob.**

I had not realized until recently that the family had actually known Mason, who was a professor of English at Gettysburg College. He wrote out that particular poem in his own hand. It is possible that my father remembered this and asked for Annie's book before he wrote out the poem, but not likely. I had the impression from Annie that her book had lain in a remote desk drawer for decades, and my father made a point of telling my mother and me that he had memorized the poem and always remembered it over the years. But the personal connection to Mason no doubt had something to do with the poem's impact on my father. It was a link to the culture of Gettysburg.

During these winter sojourns, the Saskatchewan Hollingers made frequent visits to Washington to visit Jacob, a senior clerk in the Navy Department where he had been employed since 1903. Jacob was also an ordained minister who preached periodically in the church his father had founded in 1900. Most Brethren congregations until the middle of the twentieth century had a presiding elder, colloquially known as the "ruling elder," an office Jacob held for a quarter-century in the Washington City church. Jacob and his wife, Maude, lived in a spacious home on Capitol Hill that served as a warm and secure refuge for the Saskatchewan Hollingers. Jacob understood this. His letters often reminded his siblings of the scene there by describing the physical atmosphere of the home—just where he was sitting, what the cat was doing, whether Maude had gone to bed, and what he was reading in *The Washington Star*. Today, 315 A Street SE remains an imposing brick residence just around the corner from the Folger Library and bears a plaque noting its historic status as one of the great ante-bellum homes on Capitol Hill.

In their journeys back and forth from Saskatchewan, the family often stayed in Brethren homes in Indiana, Iowa, North Dakota, and Montana. Annie kept a journal of several of these trips, describing these homes, the food they ate, and the weather they experienced. Winter always arrived in Kindersley before the Hollingers drove east and was still in command when they returned west. They frequently encountered snowdrifts and icy roads.

**Junior and Roland contemplating their car stuck in the ice and snow while traveling back to Kindersley in 1930 after spending several months in Pennsylvania.**

Transport across rivers was by ferry from the early-April thaw through the hard freeze of mid-November, but during the winters cars simply drove across the ice. On November 22, 1931, the Hollinger car was the first that winter to cross the South Saskatchewan River near the town of Outlook. There was no science to it; only an experienced ferry operator's judgment. "The ferry man says it is safe to drive across," Annie recorded in her journal. Charles drove the Packard while the others walked at a distance, fanned out, each carrying suitcases removed from the car to lighten the load, with snow falling at dusk. In one later year the snow on the Saskatchewan roads was so deep even in November that they drove west to Calgary, where they could take the paved and well-maintained highway down to Shelby, Montana, and then proceed eastward on the "highline highway," later US 2.

My grandfather died in February of their 1931-32 visit east. He was 78. He suddenly collapsed and died instantly from a heart attack while offering a prayer to open a meeting at Elizabethtown College, a nearby Brethren institution, where he was scheduled to deliver an address. Junior had driven him there and witnessed the death. "Elder Albert Hollinger," the family named him on his gravestone in Gettysburg. No "Bishop Hollinger" for them.

**This photograph of Albert Hollinger, Sr., was taken in Lancaster shortly before his death.**

My grandfather's death created a new context for his children, especially Junior, who turned 29 that summer. Junior felt more strongly an ambition he had been quietly developing to enter the ministry himself. All his siblings encouraged him, including Jacob, whose already great authority increased now that he was the family's senior member. It took a while to happen, as I describe below. But all four of the Kindersley siblings had to decide what to do next.

# CHAPTER THREE

## Out Of Canada: But To Where, And To What End?

**The Canadian Four** returned to Saskatchewan, resumed farming as before, and deliberated about the future. If their new independence issued in reassessments of their late father's record as a parent and family leader, they did not reveal them in any way accessible to me. When I heard the siblings talk about their father in later years in California, they were reserved and, to my ears, surprisingly protective. "Dad did the best he knew," one or the other of them would say. As I began to realize what my grandfather had done, I had to restrain myself from asking why he had not felt obliged to better inform himself before making some of the decisions that had affected the lives of his children so profoundly.

Any impulse the four siblings may have felt to get out of Canada fast was mitigated by the crops of 1932 and 1933, which were the best ever. The 1932 crop yielded 43 bushels per acre. Still, the market was poor. And the situation at church was a disaster. Preaching duties were taken over by Isaac Baker, the patriarch of the Brethren in Christ group that had first recruited the Hollingers to Kindersley. Baker was elderly, not much of a speaker, and prone to a literalist reading of scripture that many in the community found labored and arcane. He preached one sermon that consisted of adding up all of the "begats" in Genesis in order to determine the age of the earth. Services at the Merrington church were held intermittently for the remainder of the 1930s, whenever guest preachers passed through the area. Services were entirely discontinued in the next decade and the church edifice was torn down. In 1978 local authorities erected a monument marking its location as the earliest church of any kind to be built in that part of Saskatchewan.

Services at the Merrington church might have proceeded more regularly had Junior felt ready to take over. But he knew he needed more education. Baker's pathetic efforts in the pulpit reinforced this feeling. Junior decided in the fall of 1933 to go to Chicago, where the Brethren operated a training school for church workers as well as a seminary. He was not sure how long he would stay, but he wanted at least to spend some time there. During the summer before he

**In this photograph of the male participants in the 1933 Kindersley production of *Iolanthe*, Charles is second from left, in the back row, and Junior is second from right.**

departed, he and Charles sang in a production of the Gilbert and Sullivan operetta, *Iolanthe*. They retained warm memories of this experience, and loved to show others photographs of the performance. This event indicates how comfortable the Hollingers had come to feel, as Brethren, interacting with the Anglicans who ran the Kindersley schools and other civic institutions.

After the excitement of the Gilbert and Sullivan production and the completion of the fall harvest, Junior hitchhiked, alone and nearly penniless, to Chicago. He boarded the train only to cross the border. Depression-era customs officers were refusing to admit even US citizens unless they could afford at least a train ticket. When he got off the train after dark in Minot, North Dakota, he began to walk what is now US 2. I drove this stretch of highway myself in 2003, mindful of my father's presence there seventy years before. He walked many miles carrying a heavy suitcase. Finally he reached a house near Surrey that belonged to Deardorff relatives. He spent the night there, and the next day stood on the road again. Eventually, after getting rides through Minnesota and Wisconsin, he reached the cultural and administrative capital of the Church of the Brethren.

Junior was welcomed by the large community affiliated with the seminary, the training school, and the Brethren-operated hospital near Garfield Park. He found a job selling shoes at Sears and enrolled in an adult night school to work toward a high school diploma. He joined the choir of the large Church of the Brethren near the seminary, and always remembered singing in Handel's *Messiah*. He kept his copy of the score the rest of his life, and sometimes took it with him when he attended performances of the great oratorio. I was aware, growing up, of how hard my father struggled not to weep during the alto solo, "He shall feed his flock" (Isaiah 40:11). In November, Junior was joined by Charles, Annie and Roland who spent several weeks in Chicago before making their way again to Pennsylvania. This routine continued during the winters of 1934-35 and 1935-36. Charles and Roland found what jobs they could in Chicago, including window-washing, before and after spending a month or two in the east.

**Charles took this photograph of Junior, Annie, and Roland in Chicago in 1933.**

Junior's life took new shape under the influence of the Chicago Brethren who assured him he had real talent. He began to believe in himself for the first time. With the support of his siblings, he decided to stay on in Chicago and continue his education. Bracing experiences in the summers of 1934 and 1935 were pivotal for Junior. In the first of those summers he attended the Church of the Brethren Annual Conference at Ames, Iowa, and was thrilled to be part of the choir. Then he was sent to the tiny congregation in Vidora, Saskatchewan, to serve for six weeks as summer pastor. His first preaching experience excited him. He then joined a group of seminary students and faculty from Chicago to help lead a two-week youth camp in Arrowwood, Alberta. Again, people told him he amounted to something. After so many years of being bound to the soil, in effect, it was a new, good feeling. The next summer, Junior visited a number of churches in the upper Midwest and Canada as part of a singing and speaking team led by seminary music professor Alvin Brightbill.

Junior credited Brightbill with changing his life, especially by his repeated assurances that he would become a fine preacher. At the 1935 youth camp, again at Arrowwood, Brightbill showcased my father as an able speaker and an excellent baritone. Junior loved to sing. His favorite hymn was "God of Grace and God of Glory," a preference that I believe dated from that summer. "Grant us wisdom, grant us courage, for the facing of this hour." Photos from that summer show my father as an outgoing, convivial personality, clearly enjoying the company of other church workers. When feeling confident, Junior had a

Junior, far right, clowning for the camera in this 1935 picture of several members of the singing and speaking team the Chicago Brethren sent to churches in Alberta and North Dakota. At far left is Alvin Brightbill, the music professor who changed Junior's life.

booming voice and a hearty laugh. At six-foot-two, he was taller than most of the men around him and had great physical strength.

At Arrowwood that summer of 1935, Junior was smitten with another church worker, Berta Myers of Cando, North Dakota. This was apparently his first flirtation of any significance, and he thought she was responding well to him. He expected to pursue the relationship when he saw her again a few weeks later while traveling back to Chicago from Glacier National Park, to which he and Brightbill and several others took a detour.

**Junior and other church workers at Logan Pass, Glacier National Park, July 20, 1935.**

But when the party got to Cando, Berta was strangely distant. There is no mystery about what happened. Berta's sister, June, who knew the Hollingers well, must have alerted Berta that Albert Hollinger, Jr., had a mother and a brother who were mentally ill. Nothing was said, but Junior figured it out. He did not see Berta again for more than forty years. At that time, neither spoke of what might have been.

Another year in the company of the Chicago Brethren advanced the young man's integration into the most culturally progressive elements of the Brethren leadership. The atmosphere was different not only from the tiny congregations of Canada, but from the relatively conservative churches of Pennsylvania. The Chicago-based leaders of "the Brotherhood," as the denomination continued to call itself until the 1970s, were moving the Brethren into mainstream, ecumenical Protestantism as displayed in the *Christian Century* and as institutionalized in the Federal Council of Churches, which the Brethren joined in 1942 after strong lobbying by the Chicago leadership. By the mid-1930s at the Chicago headquarters, the Brethren were no longer a sect, but junior partners with the Methodists, the Congregationalists, and other major denominations in what then seemed an inspiring project of religious modernization. The Brethren developed the Heifer Project, in which farm families contributed heifers to impoverished and war-torn families, first in Spain, and later throughout Europe and the world. Junior sometimes went up to Evanston to hear the great Methodist preacher, Ernest Fremont Tittle.

In 1936 Junior enrolled at La Verne College, in Southern California. At 33, he had a high school diploma. He also had one hundred dollars. This was not enough to live on or to pay minimal college expenses. The President and the Dean decided to hire Junior as a part-time custodian. He got up early each morning during his first year at La Verne to clean the administrative and faculty offices. McPherson College, a Brethren institution in central Kansas, might seem to have been a more logical destination for a prairie farmer. But McPherson was almost as far from Kindersley as La Verne— about 1,700 miles driving distance. Church leaders encouraged the young people from Canada to attend La Verne, the designated institution in the Brotherhood's Pacific Coast Region, which included

Western Canada. Also, McPherson had enough students to keep it going during the depression while La Verne was barely able to maintain itself.

Charles, Annie, and Roland followed Junior to the small town of La Verne in the winter of 1936-37 and again in 1937-38. They scrambled for jobs, again, to supplement the family income. The annual winter migration was no longer to Pennsylvania, but to Southern California, and usually by way of the state of Washington where Charles and Roland worked in the orchards and packing houses owned by the Brethren in Wenatchee and Tonasket. As so often, where the Hollingers went depended on where Brethren communities were located. Although the four Hollinger siblings were all "religious" in their acceptance of Brethren teachings, they were church-centered rather than faith-centered in their conversations and in their decisions about the direction of their lives. Southern California became their new home, although not all at once. The Hollingers' decisions were slow to come.

The most important decision in the late 1930s was what to do with the farm. Related to that was what were Charles, Annie, and Roland to do with the rest of their lives. Junior, at least, had a plan. At the end of the 1938 summer the Hollingers turned over to a young neighbor the running of the farm and the obligation to pay annual installments to creditors. Forbes Webster was glad for the opportunity. He corresponded with Charles every few weeks for the next three years. Gradually, it was agreed that Webster would take over ownership, too. The summer of 1938 was the last in Kindersley for Charles, Annie, and Roland; 1933 had been the last for Junior. In the summer of 1941 the Hollingers transferred ownership to Webster. Charles and Annie returned to Kindersley to sell their horses, farm equipment, and household goods at a public auction.

That closeout event was an epic moment in the Hollinger saga, marking their transition from a life based on the traditional family farm to one supported by earning wages in a variety of disparate settings. Before I describe that moment, let me recount what else happened between 1938 and 1941.

Junior worked his way through La Verne College with a variety of jobs, especially house painting but also "smudging," the lighting and maintaining of the oil-filled "smudge pots" used to heat orange groves to protect the fruit from frosts during the winter months. Junior also did household maintenance for local Brethren families in whose homes he roomed. The College had no men's dormitory then (and did not until 1947), and male students lived around town in whatever lodgings they could find.

Through the local church he met the woman who would become his wife, and my mother, Evelyn Steinmeier Hollinger (1912-2001). Evelyn was a home economics teacher at nearby Chino High School and had learned about the La Verne Church of the Brethren from colleagues who had attended La Verne College. She found this congregation's relative liberalism and high educational level a refreshing alternative to the fundamentalist environment in which she had grown up. Evelyn disliked

**My father's yearbook photo when he obtained his B. A. degree at La Verne College, 1940.**

the evangelical style of the Church of the Nazarene. She flourished in the company of the many young adult Brethren she got to know around La Verne. She and Junior were married in late May, 1940, and were soon on their way to Chicago where my father at last entered Bethany Biblical Seminary as a divinity student. Church leaders cautioned Evelyn that she should undergo Brethren baptism in order to avoid a lukewarm welcome from some congregations. The minister who performed the wedding in the La Verne church also conducted a private baptism for my mother. She often mentioned this, assuring people that even though she was not of "Brethren background," as the tribal boundary was commonly invoked, she was fully Brethren.

**My parents in La Verne in 1940, planning their trip to Canada and Chicago.**

Junior and Evelyn got to Chicago by way of Arrowwood, where my father served as summer pastor to a congregation to which he already had close ties. While there, he drove over to Kindersley to retrieve some of his father's books, still stored away in the old house on Section 13. That one-day visit was his last time in Kindersley. As described in Evelyn's letters to several family members, that summer pastorate was a fulfilling experience for both of my parents. My father kept a journal, apparently for the only time in his life, which also registers what an enjoyable time the newlyweds were having. The community loved having the dynamic young couple around. Evelyn enjoyed the respect she suddenly received as the minister's wife. In a charming turn characteristic of the great age of radio, my mother would stop writing when the Jack Benny program came on the air, then resume writing afterwards, speculating about how her correspondents might have reacted to the program to which she knew that they, too, had listened.

It was during this time in Arrowwood that my mother conceived. She and my father seem not to have

**Junior with congregation, Bow Valley Church of the Brethren, Arrowwood, Alberta, 1940.**

been terribly disturbed by the unexpected pregnancy, judging from the cheerful tone of her letters once they arrived in Chicago. I was born the following April in the Brethren hospital at 3435 West Van Buren Street, near the seminary.

**My father holding me as an infant, July 4, 1941.**

In the meantime, Charles and Roland rented and operated a gas station in Pomona, the town next to La Verne. Annie was not regularly employed during these years, although she may have done some domestic service for local Brethren families. She did attend night school in Pomona working toward her high school diploma, which she finally earned in 1943, when she was 38. Their now-married brother Junior had departed, and the other three had to decide what to do. Hoping to stay in California, they were relieved that Webster remained willing to buy the farm. He was doing well enough that he could agree to pay the Hollingers about a thousand dollars for their equity. So, Charles and Annie drove to Kindersley to end the twenty-year Canadian adventure. Roland ran the gas station while Charles was away.

**Charles and Annie in La Verne in July, 1941, before getting into the car to drive to Kindersley for the auction of their farm equipment, horses, and household goods.**

A copy of the poster advertising the auction of July 9, 1941, has come down to me along with the Gettysburg bullets, the bottles of wheat kernels, and a trove of photographs and letters from Pennsylvania and Saskatchewan. In my hands, too, is a list of all the friends who appeared to say goodbye, a handwritten record of each item sold, and the name of the purchaser and the exact purchase price. Many of the buyers had names I recognize from the Hollingers' correspondence and the stories I later heard them tell. Webster bought two of the three horses, a black gelding for $54 and a brown mare for $29. Another neighbor bought the bay gelding for $32. A thresher brought $75, a disc $110, a tractor $210, a dresser $10, a table $6, a saw $9, a churn $2, a desk $7, and so forth. The list includes dishes, cutlery, and other items sold for as little as a few cents. A safe with the name "Albert Hollinger" painted on the front was sold for $30, and was still used in a Kindersley business in 1990 when I visited there. These dollar amounts are in Canadian currency. In 1941 a Canadian dollar was worth about $1.50 US. The auction yielded a total of slightly more than 1,000 Canadian dollars, worth approximately 1,500 US dollars. That was it, plus the small equity the Hollingers received from the land, which itself was adjusted down from the 1,000 US dollars they expected Webster to pay, taking account of the goods he purchased at the auction.

As soon as the Hollingers were gone, the economic climate on the prairies changed, and for the better. In another chronological turn of fate, Webster made a killing in the wet years and booming markets of the 1940s. He paid off all the creditors. In the 1950s he built a substantial new house on the property for himself and his family. The Hollingers rejoiced in this, and maintained regular contact with Webster, while reflecting on the ironies of their own economic relationship to the farm. As the decades witnessed more efficient farming techniques and equipment, one or two farmers could farm five or six sections, enabling profitable yields even amid the contingencies of the weather. The Hollingers arrived in Saskatchewan just as things were getting worse, and they left just as things were getting better.

**The house that Forbes Webster built for his family at the location of the old Hollinger house on Section 13.**

Charles and Annie visited Kindersley one more time, in the 1970s. They entered a "pioneer museum" filled with artifacts contributed by local pioneer families. There, in carefully curated display cases, they noticed a number of items they had carried with them from Gettysburg half a century before and then sold at the 1941 auction. Annie was dismayed that these artifacts of pioneer life were all credited to the families who bought them at the auction. Annie understood that she had been erased from Canada.

# CHAPTER FOUR

## Dispersed But Dependent

**Although the Canadian** sojourn was finally over in 1941, the lives of Charles, Junior, Annie, and Roland all continued to be affected by its legacy, individually and collectively. There were disappointments related to deficits in their childhood and adolescence. When hitting various walls, as I explain below, they were drawn back to one another for support. Their several stories remained connected in a single drama.

At first, they found new jobs, mostly as a result of a historic event half a year after the auction: American entry into World War II. Roland, at 34, was drafted early in 1942. As a conscientious objector, he entered Civilian Public Service. He was first sent to a road-maintenance camp near Santa Barbara, California, then to Castaner, Puerto Rico, where the Brethren Service Commission operated a complex of agricultural and public health programs and a hospital. Charles could not manage the gas station by himself. He obtained a job as a custodian at La Verne College. Annie took a job at the College, too, as matron of the women's dormitory. Junior and Evelyn were already in Chicago during this period, and spent the summer of 1942 in north central Wisconsin, near the village of Stanley, where my father served as summer pastor to two small Brethren congregations.

**The Kindersley Four in 1940 in La Verne on the eve of Junior's marriage to Evelyn Steinmeier. This was their favorite picture of themselves.**

The Wisconsin parsonage was a slightly updated sod house with one dirt wall. Sanitation was an outhouse. "It was a two-seater," my mother always said when she told the story, explaining it had been designed for a household with a large family. Evelyn did not much like this taste of rural, frontier life. But she and my father found that many of the families in the area raised children under these circumstances and did not think it unusual for my mother to have to manage with a toddler in such a house. The churchgoers were so taken with my father that leaders of the two congregations pledged to come up with the money to pay him if he would stay on to serve as their minister. He and my mother decided they would be better off moving on, and hoped for an assignment in a less isolated, more attractive setting. But the enthusiasm of the Wisconsin families convinced my father that he had found the right calling.

**My father with the congregation of the Mable Grove church, one of two near Stanley, Wisconsin, that he served as summer pastor in 1942.**

Junior received his divinity degree from Bethany in May 1943. Edith and Jacob managed to travel to Chicago for the event. It was the last time my father saw Jacob, who died ten years later. My parents, hauling me as a two-year-old, visited La Verne briefly that summer for the wedding of Charles to Ethel Dresher, a never-married woman nearly his age who had grown up in Surrey, North Dakota. The two met at the College, where Ethel worked as Registrar and as the small institution's entire secretarial staff.

After the wedding, my parents proceeded with me to Fruitland, Idaho, where my father had accepted a pastorate after gently putting aside earnest entreaties from the declining Canadian churches to return to the prairies and provide the ministerial leadership they had lacked since his father's death. Having written his Bethany senior thesis on "A History of the Church of the Brethren in Western Canada," my father understood there was actually no future for the Canadian churches. Young people moved away, usually to the United States. Indeed, Junior was part of a cohort of twenty-five young people from the Canadian congregations of Brethren who went to La Verne College between 1920 and 1945. Only one returned. The remnants of all the Brethren congregations in Western Canada eventually joined the United Church of Canada, in 1968.

**This carefully posed photograph of my parents and me, taken in March 1943, was designed by church officials to be shown to Brethren congregations who might want to employ my father as their minister.**

In 1943, eleven years after my grandfather's death, Charles and Annie were in La Verne, Roland was in Puerto Rico, and Junior was in Idaho. Several features of this dispersion invite elaboration.

Charles' life course from his marriage onward on was the most settled and consistent of the four. Ethel moved to a better-paying job as secretary to the local superintendent of schools, but Charles remained a custodian at La Verne College for another quarter century. During my student years there, 1959-63, I regularly saw him sweeping the classrooms and offices of the main buildings and tending to various maintenance tasks. It was a clearly bounded life, but he made a go of it. When he retired he was named an honorary alumnus of the College. Charles invested the couple's modest income wisely and in 1951 was able to build a small house for himself and Ethel on Third Street, La Verne's most attractive residential location. That same year Charles was again a source of important support for his siblings when my father suddenly decided to leave an Olympia, Washington pastorate—much more on that life-changing episode below—and to move with my mother and me to the La Verne vicinity again. Always steady and deliberate, Charles as I knew him was just as conscientious and reliable as Jacob's letters of the 1920s complimented him for being even then.

Roland's four years in Civilian Public Service gave his life a structure it had previously lacked. While in Castaner, he finally enjoyed a broadened social experience, not unlike what his brother Junior encountered in Chicago a decade earlier. Living in barracks with other men was the closest Roland ever came to the social experience of high school or college. Although the environment was heavily male, some of the senior officials and doctors at Castaner had wives, and the hospital employed a number of nurses. All were part of a single community. Several of the CPS men married local Puerto Rican women. Roland was a cook, working closely with a rotating staff of men and women in the kitchen and dining facility. For Roland, it was a dynamic scene and he found himself well liked. So long fearful and withdrawn, the youngest Hollinger was finally developing genuine friendships.

Roland wrote letters almost daily to Annie, describing the expanded society he was enjoying at last. He wrote detailed accounts of what he saw on long bicycle rides in the surrounding countryside. His letters began to show a reflective, self-aware quality that his siblings found novel and refreshing. The CPS man with an eighth grade education became the lifelong scribe to his unit. He maintained up-to-date address lists and orchestrated occasional reunions. He corresponded individually with a half-dozen or more of his CPS friends for decades. He joined the Fellowship of Reconciliation, a national organization in which Brethren, Mennonites, and Quakers cooperated with secular pacifists. When I was in Roland's company, there was hardly a day when he did not mention his CPS experience. Like the many youths adrift whose lives are given shape by military service, Roland was transformed by Civilian Public Service. He emerged in 1946 as a more focused, articulate, and self-reliant man.

Yet it was not enough to enable him to decide what to do next. At 39, he had no desire to try school and, as a conscientious objector, he was not eligible for the benefits of the G. I. Bill that paid for the education of military veterans. For the next decade Roland bounced from one job and location to another, living in Cuba for a while, working at a gas station in El Centro, California and in the orchards of Washington State, coming close to marriage in Florida then pulling back from it, and eventually finding permanence only when he moved to La Verne in the mid-1950s and was reconnected with the enduring sibling support system.

The first of Roland's many steps beyond Puerto Rico was working in another of the denomination's service enterprises, in Falfurrias, Texas. The Director of the Brethren Service Commission, M. R. Zigler, a family friend who had visited Castaner several times, was aware that Roland had no plans for himself. Zigler recruited Roland for Falfurrias, a village in Duval County near the Rio Grande border. The Brethren operated a small farming mission, organized to assist local Hispanic farmers in making better use of their land. There were no religious services. Roland wrote every day or two to Annie, describing his efforts to maintain the rather poorly equipped facilities and his disgust at the huge gap between rich and poor that he observed. He reported hearing local merchants brag about how easy it was to cheat the ignorant and uneducated farmers who came to buy goods and services. Zigler reluctantly released Roland in the spring of 1947 when he decided he wanted to travel in Mexico and Central America.

In frigid Saskatchewan, Roland had developed an ambition to live in the tropics. His time in Puerto Rico reinforced this idea, and while the climate in Falfurrias was warm, the scene was too desolate, physically and socially. Roland roamed Central America and the Caribbean for several months, then decided to settle in Cuba working a farm together with a friend he had made in Puerto Rico. But it proved hard to turn a profit and, after a year, Roland departed. He found a gas station job in El Centro, in California's Imperial Valley, but was lonely there. He went again to Wenatchee, where it was colder but he could find steady work in the orchards owned by local Brethren. He spent most of 1949 and 1950 in Wenatchee, coming across the Cascades frequently to visit my parents and me, then living in Olympia. Next, Roland moved to Florida and took jobs as a caretaker of several large estates north of Miami.

During these same years Annie was also undecided about what to do. She did not enjoy the role of dormitory matron. Many of her charges were more sophisticated about some aspects of life than she, their supposed mentor. She tried taking college courses, but felt awkward in the classroom with students half her age. She thought she might like to try teaching. My parents wrote her from Idaho encouraging her to move there, assuring her that rural school districts often employed teachers with only a high school diploma. Annie moved to Idaho in 1946 and was immediately hired as a first grade teacher in nearby Emmett. She thrived in her new role. It was her first normal, full-time job, and it paid more than the pittance she had earned as a dormitory matron. For the next two years she spent every weekend with us in Fruitland.

Fruitland was a prosperous farming community in the heart of the fertile lands where the Payette and Boise rivers flow into the Snake River near the Oregon line.

**Annie at 40, as a matron of the Miller Hall Women's Dormitory at La Verne College, 1945.**

The church's families gave my parents and me a warm welcome. The letters written by each of my parents to other family members leave no doubt that the five years in Idaho were the happiest in both of their lives. My father's congregation of 200 was large for a rural church. The Fruitland Brethren were proud of a new cinderblock church building that had been dedicated shortly before we arrived. They were proud, too, immediately after the war, when several men from the Fruitland church volunteered to take care of heifers on the ships used by the Brotherhood to transport farm animals to war-devastated Europe. The large farm families reminded my father of the social atmosphere of his youth in Gettysburg. Indeed, the church was always filled with children. In one span of only two years, the congregation sent a dozen of its young people to McPherson College. Semi-urban La Verne was closer in miles and remained the designated college for the Brotherhood's Pacific Coast Region, but Fruitland families favored McPherson, located in a traditional rural community and more protected from the cultural uncertainties they associated with California.

**The Fruitland, Idaho, Church of the Brethren, which my father served as minister, 1943-1948.**

Fruitland's main street was a Norman Rockwell classic. There was a drug store, a barber shop, a dime store, a feed store, a grocery store, and a pool hall. The church and parsonage were just across the alley from that main street, which was US Highway 30, cele-brated as part of "the Lincoln Highway," as was Gettysburg's main street. This provided a symbolic connection to my father's child-hood that he often mentioned. School was close enough for me to walk home for lunch every day. No one worried about first graders like me walking the street alone. My mother taught two classes of home economics each morning at the high school, while my father looked after me.

**My father, with me, raking and burning leaves between the church and the parsonage, fall 1944, during the happiest period of his life.**

My mother's modest income from teaching greatly helped the family's finances. Even the thriving Fruitland Brethren pre-ferred to pay the minister more in orchard produce and sacks of potatoes than in money. I can remember the many gunny sacks full of sprouting spuds in our basement, and dozens and dozens of jars of canned fruit. What I was unaware of at that time were the frustrations my parents experienced with a coal-burning furnace that was inadequate for the house and a refrigerator that leaked gas. The Fruitland parishioners, for all their good will, remained in thrall to the traditional assumption that ministers and their families did without many material things. Scripture taught that people were not supposed to live "on bread alone" (Matthew 4:4), and ministers were understood to exemplify this teaching about the value of a life of the spirit. When my parents bought a new 1946 Ford, made possible by my mother's income and a small inheritance from her parents, who both died in California that year, they felt, as never before, that they had arrived. They were living the life toward which they had been headed.

A highlight of each of our Idaho years was a two-week camping stay at Camp Stover, the Brethren retreat between the towns of New Meadows and McCall, where Summer Assembly was held, bringing together families from the several Brethren congregations in the District of Idaho and Western Montana. My father was the most popular speaker among the District's ministers. His robust baritone was always heard in the singing around the campfire. "Study War No More" was a favorite. "Gonna lay down my sword and shield, down by the riverside, and study war no more." He also liked "Jacob's Ladder" and "Sarasponda." The campfire meetings at Camp Stover are among my earliest memories.

**My father, known for his hearty laugh, in a fishing boat near Camp Stover, summer of 1947.**

I believe my parents would have remained in Fruitland for many more years—with unknown consequences for them and for the kind of person I would become—were it not for a single but persistent frustration. One older parishioner, himself an ordained minister, thought my father's up-to-date, Bethany Seminary-inspired preaching was too liberal. My father rarely mentioned hell, and did not focus on the dynamics of salvation. In keeping with the trend in the liberal Protestant seminaries of the 1940s, he preached on broad, human brotherhood themes, heavily dependent upon the Sermon the Mount section of Matthew. He avoided the sectarian affirmations that older, more conservative ministers often favored. The membership as a whole was untroubled, but my father was nettled by this one parishioner's unrelenting criticism even though for most part voiced privately. Junior was highly conflict-averse.

This one annoyance, my mother explained years later, drove my parents' decision to try another church. In 1948 we left Fruitland for Olympia, Washington, where my father became the minister of the Church of the Brethren there.

Olympia changed everything. But before I turn to that, I must recount a remarkable development in Annie's life that took place in Fruitland and I want to attend, also, to what happened to Roland in Florida.

Annie was befriended in Fruitland by Vesta Bollinger, a single woman of about the same age who was, like Annie, a first grade teacher. Vesta's family was among the earliest of the Brethren to settle in Idaho. Her brother was a much-celebrated missionary to India. When my parents and I left for Olympia in August of 1948, Annie moved into Vesta's house. From then on, the two made their home together and were always treated as a couple. This arrangement was not unusual for single women of that generation within virtually all denominations and beyond. I never heard anyone suggest that the two were romantically or sexually entangled, nor do I have any reason to think they were, nor that it matters. But what does matter is this:

**Vesta Bollinger, left, with Annie in Fruitland in 1955.**

a new bond gave Annie's life a crucial element of continuity and stability. Annie was never good at making decisions on her own. She could do little without consulting one or more of her brothers. Vesta was a clear-headed, well-organized, quiet woman for whom life seemed straightforward. Annie taught school for another decade, then became a children's librarian at the Ontario, Oregon, public library, just across the Snake River from Fruitland, where Vesta continued to teach first grade.

Roland drove to Idaho in the spring of 1950 to pick up Annie and Vesta for a trip east to attend the wedding of Edith's daughter. Edith had continued to operate her kindergarten and had become a leading churchwoman within and beyond her Presbyterian community. She was much in demand as a speaker at women's clubs in Southeastern Pennsylvania and Maryland, and was well known for her presentation, "Women of the Bible." This trip east was Annie's last visit to Pennsylvania. After the wedding she and Vesta returned to Idaho while Roland headed for Florida to look for work.

During his four Florida years, 1950-1954, Roland had successive jobs on two large estates as a caretaker, chauffeur, and general handyman. His varied experience as a farmer, cook, gas station mechanic, and maintenance worker made him a valued all-purpose employee. His letters to Annie reported the frequent turnover of other workers on his first job and the contentious marriage of the owners. Roland himself was well treated, but eventually looked for employers who were easier to deal with and less racist toward Ft. Lauderdale's black and Hispanic workers. His new job was much more satisfactory. He seemed headed for a long-term residency in Palm Beach with William T. and Mary Sisler. Roland liked to talk about driving the Sislers around in their 1953 Mercedes Benz.

William Sisler was among the heirs to the Firestone Tire Company fortune. Many years later, long after Roland had left Florida and after William Sisler had died, his widow became a leading collector of modern painting and a major donor to the Museum of Modern Art in New York.

But in 1954 Roland had an experience on the Sisler estate that precipitated his sudden departure from Florida. It was his first serious relationship with a woman. The Sislers hired an au pair for their children, a woman from France named Ginette. That is all I know about her, because once this episode was over, it was almost never mentioned in the family. To the surprise of all the Hollingers, Roland, who had never had a girlfriend, announced that he and Ginette were to be married. But a few weeks later Roland wrote that he had decided he was not stable enough, emotionally or mentally, for marriage. In anguished letters to my parents, Roland described Ginette's growing dependence on him as threatening. He was simply not strong enough to assume the role of a husband, he said. Edith visited him and counselled him not to go through with the marriage. Edith once told me that Ginette, whom Edith probably suspected of looking for a way to acquire US citizenship, "would have changed his life greatly." I have no way of knowing whether that might have been a good idea. Perhaps this lonely man of 46, who had finally managed a measure of autonomy, would have been better off taking the plunge.

**Roland in 1953 in Florida.**

Roland spoke to me only once of this episode, when he was in his eighties and feeling down. He explained how he had held back, and that even after seeing a doctor to be better prepared for a sexual relationship, he never consummated his intimacy with Ginette. "I think I'd be better off today if I'd lived a normal life," he said rue-fully. He did not say he had made a mistake by not going through with the marriage, but he acknowledged that it was a turning point in his life. He never again sought the intimate company of a woman.

Roland left Florida for Pennsylvania where he lived with the wid-owed Edith for two years while working as a laborer in construc-tion jobs. Then Edith went to Baltimore to study for an M. A. in Education at the Johns Hopkins University, obtaining it at the age of 58 and then embarking on a new career as a college professor, first, at Elizabethtown College and then, at Gettysburg College. Meanwhile, in 1956 Roland moved to La Verne where he was re-united with Charles and with Junior, who by then had a house painting business that Roland joined. The sibling bond remained the primary frame for Roland's life.

And so, too, it did, to a lesser extent, for Junior's. When my par-ents and I left Olympia just before Christmas in 1951, we went to Southern California to be near Charles and Ethel and some of my mother's relatives.

The ministry that went so well in Fruitland came to an abrupt end in Olympia. Why?

# CHAPTER FIVE

## Gathered In California In The Wake Of A Broken Ministry

My father was much appreciated In Olympia. There were no troubling malcontents. As in Fruitland, parishioners regarded him as a highly effective preacher and as a lively and responsive social companion. He played the role of Moses in a local dramatic production sponsored by the Olympia Council of Churches. He served briefly as the Chaplain of the Washington State Senate. Only a few months after arriving in Olympia he delivered the keynote address at a meeting of Brethren leaders in the District of Washington. He opened with an account of his own personal feelings about his ministry.

In the historic town of Gettysburg there stands a brick edifice, the Church of the Brethren. It is sacred to me because inside that church is the pulpit that was my father's for many years. As a boy I looked forward to the time when I would stand in a pulpit, somewhere and preach, even as my father preached. Through the years this dream, this ambition, this high aspiration has never dimmed.

The Rev. Albert Hollinger, Jr., was an animating presence at the annual Summer Assembly for the Washington congregations, held on the eastern slope of the Cascades below Mt. Rainier. He was elected the District's Moderator, the Church of the Brethren's closest approximation to the office of bishop among the Brethren in Christ. He represented the District of Washington in the national councils of the Brotherhood. His career as a minister was going very well.

Yet the social context for their new home not what my parents had anticipated. They never felt comfortable in urban Olympia. The congregation included some rural families, but most were wage earners. The tone was set by the owners of small businesses and by civil service workers in Washington's capital city. The person my parents most appreciated was the chief mechanic for the pool of logging trucks at the Simpson Logging Company's operations at Camp Grisdale, the famous timber camp to the northwest of Olympia. This man's wife ran a support program for "girls who had gotten into trouble." I was not told what that meant. The most important family—three brothers and their wives and children—owned and operated an International Harvester dealership and service facility.

**My father as minister of the Olympia, Washington, Church of the Brethren, 1948-1951.**

The parsonage, next to the church, was on a busy city street near a grocery store and across from a gas station. Weird people sometimes knocked on the door and asked for money or spiritual advice.

My parents never liked the cramped and exposed parsonage, even less hospitable than the poorly heated Fruitland parsonage. In our last year in Olympia we moved to a home my parents rented, at their own expense, several blocks away, while the congregation's Board rented out the parsonage.

Counseling parishioners about their personal problems, always an important part of a minister's work, was hard for my father because the society in which the Olympia Brethren were embedded was so different from what he had known before. After he died, my mother explained how burdened he felt by his counseling obligations. She detailed one incident that deeply affected him and actually triggered the decision to leave Olympia.

The pastor's advice was solicited by a parishioner who reported that his wife was having an affair. A private detective had established this beyond doubt. The sheer fact was striking enough, but the man's wife was then serving as the chair of the congregation's Board of Trustees. She was one of the people my father most respected, and on whom he most relied. She worked as a secretary in an Olympia law firm. There were no lawyers or doctors in the congregation, and my parents felt that to be a "legal secretary" was to amount to something special. My own recollections of this woman are vague, but I remember how respectful of her my parents were whenever she came to our home. My father simply did not know what to say to the husband, my mother explained. He was traumatized by the realization that he did not have the knowledge or emotional resources to understand and counsel this couple about their marital problems. My parents had made only a few close friends in Olympia, and one of them turned out to be an adulteress.

All this was hidden from me, of course, as was a second basis for the decision to leave Olympia. In the summer of 1951 my mother developed persistent abdominal pains. A local doctor thought it might be ulcers, but this diagnosis was never firm. I later suspected that Evelyn was one of the many people whose health had been affected by the downwind of radi-

**The Olympia Church of the Brethren.**

ation from the Hanford nuclear facility a few hundred miles to the northwest of Fruitland. I cannot be sure of this, but her symptoms were similar to others who lived in that part of Idaho in the late 1940s and who have been the subject of several well-documented studies in recent years. Be that as it may, that possibility was not considered at the time. My mother later told me that her doctors had tried to convince her that her ailment was all in her head, simply an emotional disturbance. This frightened her and my father. In later years in California, she managed to greatly reduce her discomforts by changing her diet. But when my parents left Olympia they were seeking a less stressful setting in which to figure out what was wrong. My father must have been evasive because the Board appointed a committee to talk with him about what the minutes of a Board meeting referred to as "the confused situation." It was in response to my mother's ill health that the Board accepted their popular minister's resignation on December 9, 1951. When I recently read the Board's minutes of that meeting, I noticed that they were written and signed by the very woman whose adulterous affair was so traumatic for my father and convinced my parents that Olympia was not a sustaining community for them.

Yet the emphasis on my mother's health was a way of not telling the Board about the primary cause of the decision to leave, which was my father's feeling that he simply did not want the challenge of serving a church like Olympia's. Preaching, yes, but not solving the personal problems of people living in modern society. In later years, whenever my parents said anything at all about the decision, neither mentioned my mother's health. What my father would say was along the lines of "I'm not cut out for that sort of thing." I found a sentence in one of his letters of the 1970s (answering a query from an official of the Brethren in Christ church wondering what had happened to the Hollinger family's ministerial tradition) that was as explicit as he ever was about the decision, even if still somewhat elusive: "Due to some pressures not altogether uncommon to the pastoral ministry (even among the Brethren) that were too much for me to cope with it seemed wise to turn to something else."

The Rev. Hollinger had decided to "take a sabbatical," it was said. My father continued to describe it this way for a year or two, after which it became clear he was not going to accept another pastorate. Even in the wake of Evelyn's return to reasonably good health, he had decided to leave the pastoral ministry altogether. His brother Jacob showed little sympathy. "Junior, I am worried about your vocation," he wrote bluntly in the family circle letter of early 1953. Normally, the author of each letter would remove his or her previous letter and insert a new one each time the round robin arrived, but this letter of Jacob's ended up in my parents' permanent possession because Jacob died when the packet was in their hands. Jacob had a pompous, complacent side that was evident in his comments about his own exploits and the iniquity of anyone who challenged his leadership in church affairs. But here, unusual for conversations within the family, this darker side of Jacob's personality emerged at a crucial time. My mother told me his comment hurt.

Not long after Jacob's death a yet more negative letter arrived, from Jacob's widow, Maude, scolding my father for giving up the ministry. Maude extolled Jacob's steadfast and consistent life in contrast to Junior's. Maude implied that she was voicing what Jacob really thought of his drifting brother. At about the same time, all the siblings received a copy of Jacob's will. Jacob and Maude had no children. The will directed that everything be left to Maude, but that upon her death any remaining assets were to be divided equally among Jacob's surviving brothers and sisters. When Maude died eight years later, however, the Hollingers learned that she had cut them out entirely. The pastor of the Washington City Church of the Brethren had persuaded her to leave everything, including the proceeds from the sale of the magnificent home on Capitol Hill, to the church. Edith wanted to contest this disposition, but she—the girl who would not wear the bonnet forty-eight years before—was outvoted. The others insisted they should just let it go.

The minister who had convinced Maude to give everything to the church was manifestly uncomfortable meeting me, some years later. I dropped in on him unannounced during a visit to Washington in the 1970s. I asked to see the church's Jacob Hollinger Chapel, which I knew had been built with the money Maude left in my uncle's name. As we walked into the Chapel, and I was trying to process the surprising dirt and disarray, the pastor explained that the Chapel was then being used as a storeroom.

Jacob was ungenerous about my father's decision to leave the ministry, but Charles, Annie, and Roland never hinted any disappointment. They understood. Their support was important to Junior, and to Evelyn. What had crashed was a family project. My father often spoke of the ministerial tradition stretching back to the middle of the 18th century. His own dream of having a career as a minister had taken a long time to become a reality, and had been a driving force in the movements of his siblings. It was his enrollment in La Verne College that led Charles, Annie, and Roland to begin spending winters in California rather than Pennsylvania. As each of them struggled to find a secure role in life, they gravitated to Junior as the most dynamic personality, and the one in their foursome with the career closest to the culture they had all inherited.

During the winter of 1951-52 my parents were experiencing a crisis whose dimensions they did an excellent job of concealing from me. Our move out of Olympia was abrupt and with virtually no plan for what was to happen next. We moved into a room behind the garage of the home of my mother's brother, Harold Steinmeier, in Ontario, a California town a few miles east of La Verne. My father, at 48, apparently had no idea of how he was going to earn a living. He accepted what was clearly a case of charity employment, working in my Uncle Harold's radio sales and service store. I knew my father hated the sales work he had done at Sears in Chicago years earlier, but there he was selling radios. He and my mother were also uncomfortable with the Steinmeier clan socially. Evelyn's sister and both her brothers had become Baptists. "At least they switched from the Nazarenes," my mother would say in some exasperation with her evangelical siblings. All the Steinmeiers were much too god-talky for my parents. "The Lord this, and the Lord that," my mother would mimic them.

After a few months my father started working as a sales clerk at a fruit stand in nearby San Dimas run by a Brethren family. Then he decided to take up house painting, which had been one of his ways of making money while a student. A man who spent so many years in an unpainted house on the prairie now made his living as a house painter. I never sensed that he reflected on the potentially symbolic significance of the choice. Painting was simply a trade he was good at, and he took pride in doing it well.

My father earned enough as a painter to enable us to rent a real house in Ontario from my Uncle Harold for about two years and then, in 1954, to buy our own house in La Verne. My parents' ability to purchase real estate was an accident of the economic setting of Southern California in the 1950s, so different from that of the Canadian years. Painting jobs were abundant in the rapidly growing communities of the Pomona and San Gabriel valleys. Very little down payment was required to buy a house, and interest rates were low. The total cost for a three-bedroom home in a comfortable residential neighborhood across from an orange grove was only about $7,000. My parents were now close to the large La Verne Church of the Brethren where they had been married fourteen years before, and only a few blocks from Charles and Ethel.

The town of La Verne in the 1950s was remarkably like a Protestant-centric Midwestern farming community, although citrus was the predominant crop, rather than wheat, or corn.

This label for oranges packed in La Verne was typical of the representations of the area in commercial art. The nearby San Gabriel Mountains usually served as background for the orange groves. As images of this genre go, this one is relatively true to what the scene looked like.

The business district was a single block of locally owned stores and a locally owned bank. The Church of the Brethren was only a block away to the east, and La Verne College a block away to the west. The town consisted primarily of broad, tree-lined streets with compact bungalow style stucco or frame houses with ample back yards. Thousands of acres of orange and lemon groves surrounded the town. The peaks of the San Gabriel Mountains framed the northern horizon. La Verne was socially dominated by Brethren, who had established a denominational college there in 1891 during the same era that the Congregationalists founded a college in Claremont, as did the Baptists in Redlands, and the Quakers in Whittier. The La Verne Church of the Brethren, with nearly a thousand members, was one of the largest in the Brotherhood.

La Verne was a place where my parents could feel at home. Ever since my father went there to attend college in 1936, La Verne was the closest thing he had to a home town. In the 1950s and thereafter, he was home again, living near his reliable older brother, Charles, and Charles' steady wife, Ethel. That Evelyn had grown up only a few miles to the east also helped make the scene attractive. Nestled within La Verne's large but insular Brethren community, my father remained largely impervi-

**The Church of the Brethren in La Verne, built in 1930.**

ous to the seismic economic and demographic transformation of the surrounding area, starting in the 1960s, into a bedroom community for greater Los Angeles. Tract housing developments, multi-lane freeways, and shopping malls displaced the orange groves. Smog from auto and truck emissions often hid the mountains from view.

Throughout these La Verne years, my father maintained as much distance as he could from the social and economic complexities of modern life. He did not take out a contractor's license, but relied instead on his reputation as an honest tradesman who would not bilk the people whose houses he painted. Living in a large Brethren community in a period of economic prosperity, he could manage by doing business in this way. He billed on a time and materials basis, often reducing his charges when he thought it was "fair" to do so. He never understood the need for labor unions, and lacked any sense of how contemporary businesses operated. He was "essentially a nineteenth century man," my mother once said to me, when she sensed my puzzlement.

Indeed, whenever my father did venture an opinion about the world's complexities, he tended to fall back on old maxims that troubled me for their obvious naiveté. "One should look only on the good, the true, and the beautiful," I heard him intone many times. I am sure he knew at some level that such principles could not carry one very far in the late twentieth century world, but by the time I began to understand the kind of man he was, he was no longer interested in traveling very far in that world. The barricades against modern society my father built for himself in middle age were boundaries from which he derived at least a modicum of security.

The expansive personality that emerged in the 1930s and was so evident in the 1940s was never the same again after 1951. While my mother was socially gregarious, and enjoyed meeting different kinds of people, my father was at ease only with a narrow circle of Brethren friends. In that limited circle he could be as buoyant a personality as ever. He channeled his ministerial skills into teaching an advanced Sunday school class for adults in the La Verne congregation. In that setting, his learning in Biblical scholarship was highly prized. His weekly lessons were heavily oriented to the historical context in which this or that of Paul's letters had been written, or what was the situation of the ancient Hebrews when this or that book of the Old Testament was written. He read carefully every issue of *Christian Century*. After he retired from painting, he audited seminars at the Southern California School of Theology in nearby Claremont. Once when I visited from Michigan, where I was then living, I found him studying a selection from the work of the German philosopher Hans-Georg Gadamer that had been assigned in a course on Biblical hermeneutics.

My parents made a remarkably good life for themselves in La Verne. Their income remained low, but they lived modestly. My mother bought most of their clothing and household goods at Goodwill

Industries and other thrift shops. As teetotalers, they drank only water, and sometimes milk and tea. Much of the produce they needed was grown in the family's gardens. What little traveling they did was by car. My father took one airplane trip in 1976 to a church meeting in the east, but otherwise neither he nor my mother were ever in an airplane. Annie never flew at all. Roland had flown a few times earlier in life, but not between his move to La Verne in 1956 and his death in 2000. Charles and Ethel once flew to Germany with a church group to see the Oberammergau Passion Play, but otherwise never boarded a plane, to my knowledge.

Yet, within local confines, the La Verne years were wonderful for my mother. Inspired by the popular, albeit controversial nutritionist and natural foods guru Adelle Davis, my mother managed her recurring bouts of gastrointestinal pain with a primarily vegetarian, low sodium and sugar free diet. She became the City Hostess, visiting newly arrived residents and orienting them to the town. She was a chief organizer for the city's exhibits at the Los Angeles County Fair, and was conspicuous within the Anglo population for befriending some of La Verne's Hispanic residents. She researched and wrote a book on the history of the city of La Verne, one striking feature of which was its detailed attention to the city's Hispanic community, which pre-dated

**Evelyn during the early 1960s in La Verne, while serving as the city's official Hostess.**

the influx of Anglos following the arrival of the Santa Fe Railroad in 1887. Her book also recounted the history of segregation in La Verne, which ended only in 1946 when separate schools for Hispanic and Anglo children were abolished. When she died at 88, she had almost finished another book, on the history of the La Verne congregation of Brethren. That volume was then completed by a family friend, Galen Berry, rightly listed as co-author. My mother was once named La Verne's Citizen of the Year, and upon her retirement, a grove of trees in one of the city's parks was named for her.

After ten years in the house they had first purchased in 1954, my parents bought a smaller, bungalow home with a much larger garden on Fifth Street, only two blocks from Charles and Ethel and a half-block from the church that was the institutional center of their lives. They were joined in La Verne first by Roland, whose arrival in 1956 I have mentioned, and many years later by Annie. She and Vesta moved to La Verne in 1979, presumably to live in Brethren Hillcrest Homes, a retirement and continuing care facility. But Annie was not allowed to co-habit with Vesta. The pair had not counted on that, but the rules were the rules, and Annie's brothers found a comfortable apartment for her above a garage a few doors from my parents' house. Vesta did move into an apartment at Hillcrest. Annie visited her almost every day, and Vesta was always included in Hollinger family gatherings.

By the time Annie arrived in La Verne, Roland was already living on Fifth Street, a few doors from my parents. Remarkably, he shared a home with Edith, who retired from Gettysburg College in 1968 and purchased the La Verne house in which she and Roland lived until her death seventeen years later. There was a certain irony, perhaps, in Edith's having Roland as a regular escort and companion. I doubt if she advised him against marrying Ginette in order to bring this about, but she most definitely had Roland as her own. Roland welcomed this arrangement and regularly socialized with Edith and her Presbyterian friends from nearby Claremont. He also maintained a huge, lush garden in their backyard, where he grew much of the fruit and vegetables consumed by the La Verne Hollingers.

Thus the Kindersley Four were together again, joined by the self-assured sister who never experienced the crises that defined so much of the lives of the siblings who went to Saskatchewan. All were supported by the spouses of Charles and Junior, and all lived within a short walk of each other's homes in the church-defined town to which the Kindersley Four had fled from the prairies in the 1930s. When Edith died in 1985, Annie moved in with Roland. Vesta had recently died. Eventually, Annie and Roland occupied separate apartments at Hillcrest, too, where they lived within two hundred yards of my parents and close to Charles and Ethel, who had moved there several years before.

All five siblings, the Saskatchewan Four plus Edith on the left, taken in La Verne in the early 1980s.

As the only son and only nephew, I frequently visited "the ancient Hollingers," as my children called them. It fell to me to serve as the chief witness to each of their deaths in Hillcrest, and to preside over memorial services and make related arrangements. I came to see these responsibilities as an honor. Annie lived the longest, dying at the age of 100 early in 2006. At her memorial service, I arranged for a soloist to sing "Savior, Like a Shepherd Lead Us," her favorite hymn. "In Thy pleasant pastures feed us; For our use Thy folds prepare." I never heard her utter a religious thought, but she collected clippings of devotional meditations and she was always a loyal daughter of the church and loved its music. I included no religious content whatsoever in Roland's memorial service because he told me shortly before his death at the age of 93 that for all the Brethren community's importance in his life, the religion associated with that community had given him nothing. Even in music, his tastes had long since departed from the hymns always loved by his siblings. His favorite piece of music, which he played for himself frequently, was the adagio movement of Beethoven's Second Piano Concerto.

During these later La Verne years, my mother persisted in a habit the other Hollingers tolerated as something that meant a great deal to her. She pursued friendly arguments about religion with some of the more conservative, even fundamentalist residents of La Verne whom she came to know during her extensive civic engagements. This always made me a bit uncomfortable, but I recognized it as a sign of how glad she was, as a convert, to have the progressive Brethren faith to defend. When she was dying in 2001, I became unexpectedly involved in one of these religious conversations.

My mother asked me to complete arrangements for the sale of her car to a local mechanic who had been servicing it and who, she explained, was a fundamentalist. When I went to the mechanic's service station to complete the sale, he asked if he could speak with Evelyn again. The Hillcrest hospice was only a few blocks away, so he accompanied me there and together we entered her room. She recognized him, but was too weak to carry on their old theological debates. It annoyed me to see this fellow taking advantage of her, and pushing his arguments yet again. "I know you believe in a gospel of works, Evelyn," he said, "but works depend on faith and the only reason you Brethren can do good works is because by the grace of God you have faith in Christ." I knew that my mother would not stand for this denigration of the service tradition, but she could not contest it as she neared death and could hardly speak. Here, it was my mother's voice, rather than my father's that was muted, but the tradition of Protestant thought and feeling she was trying to defend was that of the Hollingers and the Brethren. I knew some theology and had a reasonable command of the relevant scriptures (especially James 2:18, "I will show you my faith by my works," and Matthew 25:35-40, "I was a stranger and you took me in," etc.). I carried on the discussion myself. After a few exchanges, I ushered out of the room the ghost from the religious life she had fled. So it was that the atheist son defended his mother's faith over her deathbed, literally.

Who had voice—and who did not—was also at issue in my last conversation with my father, fourteen years earlier. He had always been reluctant to talk about his decision to leave the ministry and was even more reticent about the illnesses of his mother and his brother Archie. But suddenly, as he entered hospice care, he initiated a conversation about exactly these parts of his life. He even said, "David, I want to tell you about the tragedies of our family." He had never addressed me in that manner.

On that day my father managed to tell me that his life's most precious memories were from Gettysburg, when he was five or six, sitting on the buckboard's footrest between his parents' feet as the family rode home from church singing the hymn, "Amazing Grace." This surprised me. He had never mentioned that hymn. It was not in the Brethren hymnals, perhaps because it was considered too sentimental. Attending church every Sunday all through my childhood and youth, I never heard it sung in any Brethren service. I associated it with evangelicals. My father said his mother's voice was strong and pure. Listening to this hymn while sitting by her feet, Junior felt his world more secure than it ever would seem again. "T'was grace that taught my heart to fear, And grace my fears relieved.... 'Tis grace hath brought me safe thus far, And grace will lead me home."

But he could not continue. He was repeatedly overcome. He could say no more about his mother, or about his ministry, or any of the other things I gathered he wanted to convey to me. I wondered if hidden behind his favorite saying, "Look only on the good, the true, and the beautiful," there was a vivid sense that everything else was just too painful. I suggested that he might be able to write something out. I left a pad and pencil for him. He died two weeks later without having written anything. Yet several weeks earlier, when he realized he was going to die, he wrote out the poem alluding to "ineffable words" that could be uttered only in an afterlife. Among the saddest moments of my own life have been those last few hours with my father, when he wanted to tell me important things long withheld, but could not. Whatever burdens he carried to the very end were so heavy that he could only weep. "Thou art a soul in bliss," King Lear said to his loving child,

> but I am bound
> Upon a wheel of fire, that mine own tears
> Do scald like molten lead.

Somehow, Albert Hollinger, Jr. had hit a wall. His three Saskatchewan siblings came up against barriers, too, even if less sharply defined. But he had traveled the farthest from where they all found themselves after their own father's death. Junior had taken the most risks, and suffered the deepest disappointments. I have often wondered what might have happened to him, and to his siblings, without the help they gave to one another as they navigated their many transitions. All showed great resilience, given their circumstances, and they drew strength from one another. I came to admire the success with which they built lives for themselves, even if those lives were different from the ones I could imagine each leading had they been endowed with more abundant resources when they were young. The more fully I understood what had happened to them the more amazed I was at the equanimity they all projected most of the time. It sometimes seemed to me that my grandfather had deprived them not only of many benefits that most of their contemporaries enjoyed, but that he had managed to rob them also of a capacity for anger, for resentment, for attributing their difficulties to something other than fate, or chance. But I finally came to respect their emotions. Whatever enabled the measure of peace they achieved, it was a peace they had earned.

# Genealogical Appendix

**My grandfather's parents** were Adam Hollinger (1829 -1871) and Maria Dutrey Hollinger (1830 -1905). My grandmother's parents were Ephraim Deardorff (1822-1895) and Annie Lott Deardorff (1827-1924).

See "family tree" below:

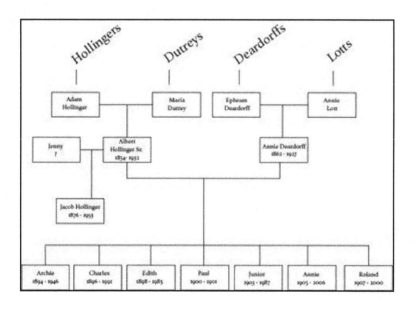

CPSIA information can be obtained
at www.ICGtesting.com
Printed in the USA
FSHW020042290519
58518FS